# SPECTACULAR SCIENCE

# 7

## FOR

## YEAR OLDS

## ILLUSTRATED BY AL MURPHY

# GLENN MURPHY

MACMILLAN CHILDREN'S BOOKS

Published 2021 by Macmillan Children's Books
an imprint of Pan Macmillan
The Smithson, 6 Briset Street, London EC1M 5NR
*EU representative*: Macmillan Publishers Ireland Ltd, 1st Floor,
The Liffey Trust Centre, 117–126 Sheriff Street Upper,
Dublin 1, D01 YC43
Associated companies throughout the world
www.panmacmillan.com

ISBN 978-1-5290-6526-8

Text copyright © Glenn Murphy 2021
Illustrations copyright © Al Murphy 2021

1 3 5 7 9 8 6 4 2

A CIP catalogue record for this book is available from the British Library.

Printed and bound by CPI Group (UK) Ltd, Croydon CR0 4YY

MIX
Paper from
responsible sources
FSC® C116313

# SPECTACULAR SCIENCE

# 7 FOR YEAR OLDS

FROM SEAN
MURPHY (AGED 7)

BY GLENN MURPHY
(AGED 47)

THIS IS <u>NOT</u> NICE.

# CONTENTS

# TEETH, CLAWS, AND DINOSAURS

# WHY DO ANIMALS HAVE TWO EYES, BUT NEVER THREE?

Most animals have two eyes because their bodies develop in a balanced way – with bits on one side of the body or face (arms, legs, eyes, ears) neatly mirrored on the other. If they only had one leg, they might fall over or run in circles forever!

**Okay – so I get why animals need balanced *bodies*. But why do they need balanced *heads*? Why not two eyes on one side of the head, and none on the other?**

Well, that's partly down to how heads and eyes develop and grow, but mostly down to how animals *use* them.

Before they're born or hatched, most animals transform from single egg cells into ball-like bundles called **embryos**. As animal embryos grow they fold and split into halves, with a left side and a right side*. From that point onwards, almost every body part (leg, foot, rib, eyeball, nostril) that emerges and grows on the left side appears on the right side at the same time. So what you end up with is an animal with two mirrored halves, or what scientists call **bilateral symmetry**.

**Symmetry** helps ensure the animal can move in a balanced way, look (or listen) both ways for predators or prey, and gives them at least one "spare part" – should an eye, ear, or limb get damaged.

Some animals, though, break the symmetry rule. Some flat fish – like flounder – swim on only one side, near the sandy sea floor, to hunt and hide from

......................................................................

* All animals with *backbones* do this. But others, like starfish and jellyfish, split like big, round cheeses or pizzas – with five, six, or seven segments all mirroring each other instead!

predators. Over thousands of years of this behaviour, evolution has been at work. So now *both* the flounder's eyes have shifted to the side it keeps uppermost. In other words, the flounder has two eyes on one side of its head, a bit like a Picasso painting!

And though animals with **three** working eyes are rare, some fish, frogs, and lizards do have three eyes. Including one rare, ancient, and tough-as-nails reptile called the **tuatara**.

## Tuatara? Never heard of it. What's that, then?

Tuataras are small, iguana-like reptiles native to New Zealand and its offshore islands. Though they look like big lizards, they are actually not lizards at all. They are the last surviving members of group of animals called **Rhynchocephalia**, which first appeared on Earth around 240 million years ago. The indigenous Māori people of New Zealand call them tuatara. Their official, scientific name is *Sphenodon*.

## Sven-odon? Sounds like a Swedish dinosaur.

Ha! *Sphenodon* means 'wedge-shaped teeth' in ancient Greek. But while they're not actually dinosaurs, sphenodons – or tuataras – have been around since the age of dinosaurs. They first walked the Earth **40 million** years *before* the Jurassic period, when stegosaurs and diplodocuses came along, and almost **100 million** years before tyrannosaurs and velociraptors.

Tuataras turned out to be tougher than their larger, scarier, dino-cousins. While most of the dinosaurs died out in two waves – during the Triassic-Jurassic extinction (200 million years ago), and Cretaceous-Tertiary (66 million years ago) extinction – the tuatara survived them both.

**Why did the dinosaurs die, but the tuatara didn't?**

Hard to say for sure. But it could be that the tuatara's smaller size and burrowing behaviour helped it survive the asteroid impact and climate change that killed off the bigger dinos. And its diet of frogs, lizards, and the eggs of other animals may have helped it scrape by while larger predators and herbivores ran out of food.

**Did its third eye help it survive? Why does it even have one?**

Good question. The tuatara's third eye – or **parietal eye** – sits in a socket on the top of its skull, just beneath the skin. You can see it clearly in babies (or hatchlings). But by the time they are four or five months old, the third eye is covered over with thicker scales. Like its other two eyes, the third eye has a lens, a retina, and a nerve leading to the brain.

But since it is covered over, the third eye can only sense vague patterns of light and shadow – not shapes, colours, and movements.

## Couldn't it just do that with its normal eyes?

Great question! Since the third eye is more open in hatchlings, maybe it helps tuatara babies to avoid predators attacking the burrow from above. Or maybe it picks out different frequencies of light to its other eyes – using patterns of polarized light from the sun to help it navigate, as some salamanders do. Some species of frog, lizard, and bird have third eyes beneath the skin, too – but none as obvious and active as that of the tuatara. Maybe all these animals use their third eye the same way, or maybe they use them differently, or not at all. The truth is, we don't really know. Hopefully, tuataras will be around long enough for us to study them and find out.

## Okay – so if animals can have three eyes, then

**could they have *more* than three eyes, but still an odd number? Like five eyes, or seven eyes?**

In theory, yes. Though we don't see them around now, at least one prehistoric animal that we know of had five eyes. It was called ***Opabinia***, and it was a soft-bodied, ocean-dwelling animal that lived in the **Cambrian period**, around **500 million** years ago.

From looking at fossils from that time, it seems that evolution went a little wild – experimenting with all kinds of weird and wonderful body shapes. There were spiky worms, feathery slugs, and animals so weird you couldn't tell which end was which.

Sadly, a series of massive extinction events followed – possibly caused by the eruption of enormous super-volcanoes, and the triggering of an ice age that turned the planet into a giant snowball. Together, these extinctions killed off over 98% of the weird and wonderful animals of the Cambrian and Ordovician periods – including the strange, five-eyed *Opabinia*.

If those extinctions hadn't happened, there could well be **five-eyed**, **seven-eyed**, even **thirteen-eyed** animals wandering the oceans right now. And who knows – on some other planet, there may well be . . .

**Cool!**

# TUATARA FACTS

● Here's a photo of a tuatara (*Sphenodon*), looking quite pleased with himself.

- Tuataras have **no eardrums or earholes**, only sound-sensing blobs of fatty tissue inside their skulls.

- Tuataras have **50% more DNA** in their cells than humans, and are evolving faster than any other known vertebrate (an animal with a backbone).

- Threatened by habitat loss and invading Polynesian rats, tuataras disappeared from mainland New Zealand in the 1700s, surviving only in the offshore islands.

- In 2005, researchers re-released a group of captive tuataras into a wildlife sanctuary area on New Zealand's north island, where they now seem to be breeding and surviving well. Hooray!

- To the indigenous Māori people, the tuatara are respected **Ariki** (god forms), and thought to be messengers of **Whiro – the god of death and disaster.**

- Unless you're an expert, don't try to handle a tuatara – they **bite hard** and **do not let go**!

# WHY DO SOME BIRDS FLY, BUT OTHERS DON'T?

Although all living birds have feathers and wings, some have adapted for walking, running, swimming, and diving – all of which are far less effort than flying. And depending on where they live – and who or what is hunting them – some birds simply don't *need* to fly. So why bother?

**So penguins don't need to fly because they can swim instead?**

Right. Over long stretches of time – anywhere from hundreds to millions of years – animal species adapt to fit their environment. New, mutant varieties pop up. Some shapes and behaviours do better than others, and the ones best suited to survival (and having babies) become the 'new normal' for the species. Biologists call this **natural selection**, and it explains how pretty much every animal species came to look the way it did.

So while swifts and swallows use their wings to swoop and flap through the skies, penguins use theirs for swimming, diving, and hunting in the Southern Ocean. Other flightless birds – like emus, ostriches, and cassowaries – became adapted to running through grasslands and forests, grew too big to take off, and now only use their wings for balance or mating displays.

And those are just the *best-known* species of flightless bird. There are also **flightless ducks**, **flightless coots**, even a **flightless parrot**. In the past – right up to 150 years ago – there were many, many more.

## So if they don't need to do it, why do birds fly at all?

Good question. Let's think about that. First up – what were birds before they were birds?

## Errr – dinosaurs?

Right. Small, two-legged dinosaurs with long legs and stubby arms. From looking at dinosaur fossils from around the world, we know that a good number of them, large and small, evolved feathers long before they could fly. Probably to keep warm, or to show off and attract mates – the way peacocks and parrots still do.

For a while, these stubby-armed, feathery reptiles ran around like chickens, dodging predators, pecking at seeds and fruit, or hunting insects, lizards, frogs, and fish in the forests and grasslands of the Cretaceous period (145 to 66 million years ago).

**So why did they start flying, and how did they do it?**

Biologists believe that flight developed many times and in many different species of dino-bird[*]. No one knows for sure, but it may have started with rare mutants that had bigger forelimbs (arms) and wider feathers.

Some of those mutants took to running up trees to escape predators and build nests. These clever proto-birds could avoid the ground entirely by gliding from

[*] It also evolved in flying insects, flying fish, and flying mammals (bats, sugar gliders, and flying squirrels). But that's a whole other story . . .

tree to tree, and those with the widest, strongest wings eventually learned to swoop, flap, and extend their glides into proper, sustained flight.

Other big-armed dino-mutants were probably more like chickens and game birds – running, jumping, and flapping to escape predators. Over time, those clumsy jumps and flaps turned into continuous flapping – allowing them to cover long distances before returning to the ground.

For a while, this seemed to give small, flying dinosaurs (now called birds) an advantage over their larger, ground-dwelling cousins. While practically all other dinosaurs died out, a good number of bird species survived the **K–T extinction event** 66 million years ago, and they have been doing pretty well ever since. There are 10,479 different bird species alive today. Of these, around 60 – like emus, kiwis, and penguins – are flightless.

**Okay. But why are almost all the flightless birds in places like Australia, New Zealand, and Antarctica?**

Well spotted. In short, because **remote islands create lazy birds** that tend to **stay put**.

Biologists *used to* think that ostriches, emus, and other flightless birds all shared the same ancestor – meaning that they all evolved from one flightless species. But by studying the DNA of everything from penguins to kakapos (flightless parrots), we know now that flightlessness has developed many different times, in many different species. So while ostriches evolved from a flightless ground bird, penguins may have evolved from an entirely flightless wading bird (shore bird) or seabird.

Why remote islands and ice sheets? Well, flying takes a *lot* of energy. It also takes a good amount of muscles to maintain the huge flight muscles that anchor a bird's forearms (wings) to its breastbone (or keel). If a bird *can* avoid flying – by swimming or avoiding predators without it – then it can save energy, eat less, and generally survive better.

For this reason, birds settling on remote islands (or places where there were few natural predators) tend to develop longer legs, stubbier wings, and smaller flight muscles. They settle into life without flight, safe in their remote island paradise.

Until, of course, some invading animal or human settles there. Then the flightless birds are in major trouble. This is why most flightless bird species have already gone extinct. Including the plump, trusting dodo of Mauritius, and the giant elephant bird of Madagascar. Sadly, throughout history, humans and helpless animals have not mingled well.

**Okay – last question . . . can I have one of those? Y'know, as a pet?**

Not a great idea, I'm afraid. Large flightless birds like ostriches and cassowaries make unwilling and dangerous pets, while smaller ones like kiwis and kakapos would almost certainly become lunch for the most vicious and enthusiastic bird-murderers of all time . . . domestic cats.

In the UK alone, house cats kill over **27 million** birds per year. In the USA, it's more than **2 billion** birds per year. And that's *flying* birds, with some hope of escape. So let's leave the kiwis and kakapos where they are – happy and free in the (relatively) cat-less wild.

# FLIGHTLESS BIRDS (PAST AND PRESENT)

● **Kakapos** are large, nocturnal, flightless parrots native to New Zealand. They are fiercely curious, excellent climbers, and can jog for miles through the forest without stopping.

● **Cassowaries** are large, flightless birds related to emus, found in New Guinea and parts of Australia. They have black feathers, blue necks and faces, and lethal, knife-like claws on their three-toed feet. They jump, kick, and slash with their claws, making them dangerous to humans.

- **Dodos** were fat, flightless, pigeon-like birds native to Mauritius, a remote island east of Madagascar. Dutch sailors first arrived in Mauritius in 1598, and hunted the trusting dodos by walking up to them and clubbing them on the head. The last one was seen in 1662.

- **Elephant Birds** were enormous, ostrich-like birds from Madagascar. They stood 3 m (10 feet) tall and weighed over 700 kg (1,500 lb). They were hunted to extinction by human settlers, somewhere between 300 and 800 years ago.

- **Terror Birds** were massive, meat-eating birds that roamed South America between 60 and 2.5 million years ago. They replaced tyrannosaurs and other dinosaurs as the largest land predators on the continent, until cats, bears, and other mammals arrived and out-competed them. Luckily for us, they went extinct at least a million years before the first modern humans walked the Earth.

THIS IS NOT NICE.

# WHY ARE THEY CALLED 'SEA LIONS' WHEN THEY'RE NOT ACTUALLY LIONS?

Because we group and give names to living things in lots of different ways, and appearance is just one of them. And although lions and sea lions may *look* very different, they are quite similar in other ways.

**Come on! Sea lions are nothing *like* lions. Lions don't have flippers, for a start! They probably can't even swim!**

Actually, lions *can* swim. All cats can. Most of them just don't like to.

**Okay – but sea lions don't have big manes or claws . . .**

No, but they do have furry bodies, sharp teeth, and whiskers. Along with many other features that you may not see at first glance.

**So how *do* we choose names for animals, if it's not about how they look?**

Great question. Sometimes, of course, we *do* group and name animals based on how they look. **Flat-headed cats**, **black-footed cats**, and **rusty-spotted cats** have slightly different shapes and colours, and their names reflect these differences. But they are still similar enough to each other that we call them all **cats**.

Other species, though, may be named for where they **live**, what they **eat**, or how they **behave**.

**Sand cats**, **wild cats**, **jungle cats**, and **Chinese mountain cats** are all unique **species**, named for the **habitats** they live in. As are **Arctic hares**, **grass snakes**, and **swamp sparrows**.

**Fishing cats** are named for what they hunt and eat (you guessed it – fish). The same goes for the **anteaters**, **bee-eaters**, **crab-eating raccoons**, and the **Goliath bird-eater**<sup>*</sup>.

Many animal species are named for how they **move**. These include **flying fish**, **jumping spiders**, and **burrowing owls**. Others are named for how big or small they are compared to similar animals of their kind. Hence, **giant squid**, **dwarf hamster**, and the (sadly) extinct **giganotosaurus**. A few are even named after mythical creatures they seem to resemble: **vampire bat**, **komodo dragon**, **common basilisk**.

The point is, animals can be named and grouped in lots of different ways. Some more accurately than others.

**Can you do that for any two animals, then? Compare how they're the same, how they're different, then decide if they should have the same name?**

Absolutely. In fact, that is exactly what scientists have done for most of the known animal species on the planet. Grouping and naming animals based on common

..................................................................................

* The largest bird-eating spider in the world. It lives in the rainforests of South America, should you wish to find it (or avoid it forever).

features is known as **taxonomy**. And for centuries, grouping and naming was pretty much all that **biologists** (or **naturalists**, as they were once called) actually did.

Here is how it works:

If two animals are the same in just about every way, they are assumed to be the same **species**. A **species** is a group of animals that can happily live, thrive, breed together, and have babies that look much the same as their parents (well, to other species, anyway).

**Asian elephants**, **moon jellies**, and **blue whales** are all unique animal **species**.

If two animals are the same in *most* ways, but different in a few, then they are classified as different species within the same animal **family**. So **polar bears, grizzly bears and pandas** are all species within the animal **family of bears** (or Ursidae).

These animals live in very different places (the Arctic, North America, Asia), eat slightly different things (seals, berries, bamboo), and come in three different colours (white, brown, black-and-white). But they are all big and furry with stubby tails, lumber around on all-fours, but stand up on their hind legs if needed. So they are all grouped into the family of **bears**. Other animal families include **cats** (Felidae), **dogs** (Canidae), **weasels** (Mustelidae), and **dolphins** (Delphinidae).

## Cool. So what are the biggest groups of animals you can have?

Well, many animal **families** (like bears and weasels) can be grouped into larger animal **orders**, like **carnivores**, **rodents**, **bats**, and **primates**\*.

**Orders** can be grouped into even larger animal **classes** – like **mammals**, **birds**, **reptiles**, **amphibians**, **insects**, **crustaceans** (crabs and lobsters).

**Classes combine to form even bigger groups called phylums** (or more properly, phyla). These include **molluscs** (slugs, snails, octopuses, and squid), **arthropods** (insects, spiders, crustaceans), and **chordates** (things with spines or spinal cords – we mammals are in this one).

Finally, each **phylum** – which can contain many classes, orders and families, and hundreds or thousands of unique species – can be placed into one of six **kingdoms**.

The **kingdom** is the largest group of living things you can get. As of 2020, we have not found any living organism that does not fit into one of these kingdoms (though that *could* change, if we ever found an alien life form). The six kingdoms are:

---

\* Which includes lemurs, monkeys, gorillas, orangutans . . . and humans!

**ANIMALS** (big, complex creatures that eat plants, fungi, other animals, or rotting bodies/vegetation)

**PLANTS** (living organisms – large or small – that get energy directly from sunlight)

**FUNGI** (this group – which includes yeasts, moulds, and mushrooms – is neither plant nor animal, and does *not* get energy from sunlight. Instead, they digest and absorb nutrients from their environment. A few live on or *inside* plants and animals)

**PROTISTS** (tiny, single-celled organisms that live in water, or inside plant and animal bodies)

**BACTERIA** (as above, only they are typically even smaller and simpler, and can live more or less anywhere there is light and food)

**ARCHAEA** (ancient, bacteria-like organisms that may have been the first on Earth. These things can survive in super-salty lakes, and in super-hot volcanic vents!)

## So how are lions and sea lions the same? What groups are they in?

Well, they are both **big, complex creatures that eat other creatures** (antelopes and zebras for the lion; fish, krill, and the occasional penguin for the sea lion). That puts them squarely in the **kingdom Animalia (or animals)**. And they both have stiff **backbones** and **spinal chords**, which makes them part of the **phylum Chordata** (or **chordates**).

They are both covered in **thick hair (or fur)**, and the **females give birth to live young**, and feed them with **milk** made in special **mammary glands**. This means both lions and sea lions are part of the animal **class Mammalia (mammals)**.

Also, since they both **eat the flesh of other animals**, and have sharp, cone-shaped **canine teeth** for that very purpose – they are in the **order** of mammals known as **Carnivora** or **carnivores**. Now here's where things get interesting . . .

There are 12 **families of carnivores. Nine** of these families live on land – these are **cats, canids (dogs), bears, hyenas, weasels*, skunks, raccoons, mongooses, and civets**.

......................................................................................................................

\* This family also contains badgers and otters. So in a way, badgers are giant, burrowing weasels, and otters are playful water-weasels!

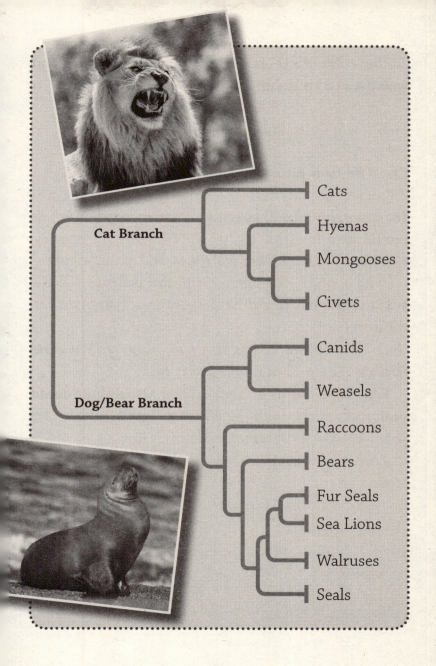

Cat Branch

Cats

Hyenas

Mongooses

Civets

Dog/Bear Branch

Canids

Weasels

Raccoons

Bears

Fur Seals

Sea Lions

Walruses

Seals

The other three families – **seals**, **sea lions and walruses** – rest and breed on land, but hunt and feed at sea. So this is where lions and sea lions split – they are in different animal **families**.

**Cool! So how many animals are in each family?**

There are around **300 species** of carnivore spread across the 12 carnivore families.

Some families – like **walruses** and **palm civets** – only have **one** living species (i.e. **the walrus**, and the **palm civet**) but might have contained many more in the past.

Other families – like the **cat**, **dog**, and **weasel** families – have 30 or more species *each*.

**Sea lions** are in a family called **Otariidae** (**eared seals**, or seals with visible ear-flaps!). There are about **15** species of eared seal and sea lion.

True, none of them would do too well flopping around after antelope on the Serengeti plains of Africa. But maybe you can see now how they earned the title 'lions of the sea'!

# TRY IT YOURSELF:
# FIND IT, NAME IT, KNOW IT

Make a chart of the 6 main groups of animals:

**Invertebrates** (which includes insects, earthworms, jellyfish, and crustaceans)

**Reptiles** (snakes and lizards)

**Amphibians** (frogs, newts, and salamanders)

**Fish** (bony fish, sharks, and rays)

**Birds** (hawks, sparrows, and blue tits)

**Mammals** (cats, dogs, mice, and moles)

Spend some time outdoors searching for examples of each group, starting with a magnifying glass to help you locate the smallest animals.

Try to find 2 or 3 examples from each animal group, then research a local citizen science project, like **The Great Backyard Bird Count**, to report your findings.

# WHY DO ELEPHANTS HAVE BIG EARS?

You might think elephants have big ears so they can hear better. But in fact, their huge, flappy ears evolved for a quite different purpose. Which just goes to show: you can't judge a book by its cover – looking a little closer can reveal a much bigger story.

**So elephants can't hear that well?**

Actually, elephants have pretty good hearing. They do have trouble hearing high-pitched sounds (like mouse squeaks and twittering birds). But on the flipside, they can hear low-pitched sounds that are below the hearing range of most humans, in what is called the **infrasound** range. Because of this, they can use rumbling, booming infrasound calls to hear and recognize other elephants **more than a mile (1.5 km) away**.

But that's not why they have big ears.

**It's not? But what else could huge ears be *for*?**

Let's think about that for a minute. Elephant ears aren't just big – they are *enormous*. The ear of an adult African elephant can measure **2 m (6 feet)** from top to bottom, and weighs over **45 kg (100 lb)**. Which means **one elephant ear is probably taller and heavier than you are**.

**Whoa . . .**

Their ears are also wide and flat, and do little to funnel sounds towards their eardrums like the hollow, cone-shaped ears of a cat, dog, or fox. Sure, they do help focus sound a bit. But not enough to warrant a **six-foot, 100-pound earlobe**.

So if they are not for funneling sounds, then what else *could* they be for?

**I dunno. Showing off, maybe? Waving at other elephants?**

29

Not a bad guess. Other animals *do* grow big teeth, noses, ears, and tails in order to send signals to mates or rivals. Think of the fan-like tail of a peacock. Or the huge, dangly nose of the proboscis monkey. Biologists think elephants may use their ears this way, too – flapping them at partners to communicate interest, or fanning them out to make their heads look bigger and scarier before a fight (as if they weren't big and scary enough already!).

But that's not quite the whole story. Because elephants don't just have massive ears so they can *look* cool. They have them so they can *stay* cool.

**Eh? How does that work?**

You know what happens when it snows, and you go outside to make snowballs and snowmen . . . only you forget to put your hat and gloves on?

**Yeah, I've done that. Your hands and face get cold, and they go all blotchy and numb. After a while, you can't feel your fingers, your nose, or your ears.**

Right. That's because those are all sensitive places where your blood flows quite close to the surface of the skin.

So you **lose heat faster** from your fingers, nose, ears and face than you do from, say, your arms, legs, belly, or back. We wear hats and gloves to **keep that heat in**, and keep our bodies warm.

But we don't wear woolly hats and gloves to the beach in summer*, as if we did, we would overheat. Instead, we peel off layers of clothing, expose more of our skin to the air or water, and release heat back into our environment as best we can.

Elephants live in very hot places. So their massive ears help them to release heat from their bodies, keeping them cooler in the scorching, afternoon sun. Those huge ears are like massive fan blades with blood vessels running everywhere inside. The extra surface area helps them exchange heat between their bodies and the air outside.

Incredibly, biologists have learned that elephants can even **control** the flow of blood **to and from their ears** (and to other, thin patches of skin found throughout their massive bodies). When elephants flap their ears, they cool the **outside** of their bodies by sending wafts of air backwards, towards their flanks. But the flapping also cools the blood **within** the ears, which flows back into the body, cooling the elephant's **insides**, too.

........................................................................
* Unless, perhaps you live in coastal Scotland, where you can still freeze your bottom off at the beach in June . . .

## So elephants have big ears to help them cool off?

Exactly. In fact, you could say that elephants have built-in **ear-conditioning**. Hahaha.

## Groan. Dad joke.

Sorry – couldn't resist it. Anyway – this ear-conditioning idea could explain why African elephants have much bigger ears than Asian ones. African elephants live in the open plains and grasslands of Africa, where the scorching sun beats down all day long, and shade can be hard to find. They need ear-conditioning to combat the relentless heat.

Asian elephants, however, live in the wetter, shadier jungles of Southeast Asia. So they do not need the huge, flappy ears of the African elephant.

*African elephant*

Asian elephants are also a little smaller, and a great deal easier to catch, tame, and train. Unfortunately, this is one of many reasons why the Asian elephant is now an **endangered species**.

## Endangered? What does that mean?

There are currently over **400,000** elephants roaming the plains and grasslands of Africa. Conservation biologists – scientists who study and protect natural resources like land, water, air, and wildlife – say the African elephant is also an **endangered species**, with numbers expanding in some areas, and falling in others.

But Asian elephants' numbers have **halved** over the last 75 years alone, and there may be fewer than **40,000** elephants left in the jungles of Asia today.

*Asian elephant*

## Why? What's happening to them?

*We* are. Humans have been hunting, capturing, and training Asian elephants for over 4,000 years. In ancient times – before tanks, trucks, and trains came along – elephants were ridden into war, used to transport heavy goods between villages and towns, or trained to clear forests and carry logs for building.

As more and more of their forest habitat was destroyed, elephants were pushed into smaller and smaller pockets of forest, bringing them into conflict with each other and with the humans building their homes in cleared forest. Thousands of wild elephants were hunted and shot just to make humans feel safer. Thousands more were hunted for the valuable ivory in their tusks.

These days, the hunting of elephants is against the law in most countries. But still, the illegal hunting (or poaching) continues. And while they are no longer ridden into battle, Asian elephants are still used to move trees that have been cut down (logging), transport, and entertaining tourists in countries such as **Thailand**, **Myanmar**, and **India**.

**That's so sad.**

It is. Very. But thankfully, international organizations like the **World Wildlife Fund** and the **Wildlife Conservation Society** are working hard to help protect elephants in both Africa and Asia. By arresting hunters and poachers, setting up protected lands where no humans can settle, and educating local leaders and peoples on the importance of protecting these majestic creatures, they have helped the African elephant recover to healthy numbers in many parts of southern and eastern Africa.

With more efforts like this, we may be able to save the Asian elephant, too.

# WHY ARE THERE NO ARCTIC SNAKES AND SPIDERS?

There are no Arctic snakes because reptiles are 'cold-blooded' animals that have a tough time keeping their bodies from freezing in sub-zero temperatures. You might *think* that would rule out Arctic spiders, too. But in fact, there are over 100 species of spider living north of the Arctic Circle, and they have come up with some very clever ways of staying warm . . .

**Wait a minute – there is such a thing as an Arctic spider?**

There is indeed. One species – the **Arctic wolf spider** (**Pardosa glacialis**) proudly bears that title, and many,

35

many more make their home in freezing, northern climates – including sheetweavers, dwarf spiders, and crab spiders*.

## So why are there spiders but no snakes up there?

Snakes are **reptiles**, and reptiles are **cold-blooded** (or **poikilothermic**) animals. By this, we mean that their body temperature tends to be similar to that of air or water around them, and they have **little or no ability to maintain their internal body heat** if the external temperature goes down. All living** reptiles – including snakes, lizards, turtles, and crocodiles – are cold-blooded. Fish and amphibians are cold-blooded, also.

The opposite of cold-blooded is **warm-blooded** (or **homeothermic**).

Warm-blooded animals can control their body temperature in different ways, keeping their insides more or less the same temperature – even when the outside temperature is way below zero, or climbs above 38°C.

**All birds are warm-blooded**. Which is how **snowy owls**, **Arctic terns**, and **emperor penguins** can survive

......................................................................

* Not to be confused with *spider crabs*, which are crabs that look like spiders, rather than the other way around!

** Though many dinosaurs may have been warm-blooded – we'll get to that later.

at the ice-capped poles of our planet. **All mammals are warm-blooded**, too. Which explains **Arctic hares**, **Arctic foxes**, and **polar bears**.

But **snow cobras** and **Arctic anacondas**? Not so much. There is one species of **garter snake** that can survive temporary freezing – sometimes, with as much as 40% of its body fluids turning to ice! These can live *close* to the Arctic, in parts of Canada and Alaska. But even *they* cannot tolerate polar life year-round.

**So are spiders warm-blooded, then?**

Actually, no. Like their ocean-dwelling, **arthropod** cousins – crabs, lobsters, and shrimp – land-based spiders are **cold-blooded** animals that depend on their environment for warmth. But in spite of that drawback, at least **100 species** of spider have adapted to survive the freezing temperatures north of the Arctic circle – in northern Canada, Greenland, Scandinavia, and Russia.

**Then how did *they* adapt? Did a spider just wake up one day and sprout a hairy coat, or learn how to build a burrow?**

No, they almost certainly did not. Like all animals, spiders adapt slowly over **hundreds**, **thousands**, even

**millions of years** – through the process of **natural selection**.

The first spiders evolved around **400 million years ago** – 200 million years before the first **dinosaurs**, and nearly 300 million years before **snakes**. As they spread out to occupy the land and became separated by mountains, valleys, and rivers, different groups or families of spiders started to form. In the beginning, these distant spider families would have looked much like each other.

But here's the thing – every time an animal has babies (or as scientists call them, offspring), **those babies will vary a little from each other, and from their parents**. One might be a little bigger and hairier, the other a little smaller and smoother. One might have longer legs, another, a slightly longer body.

If the climate and environment stays the same, and the things they eat (or that eat *them*) remain unchanged, then none of these little differences matter. But if something changes – the climate gets warmer or colder, a food source disappears, or a new predator shows up – then having a slightly hairier body, or slightly longer legs, could make the difference between a long, happy life and certain death.

Since only survivors have offspring, the animals best adapted to their environment tend to become more common over time (while their less well-adapted brothers, sisters, and cousins die out). In this way, **two or more different species can develop from a single, founding family**, and species living in separate populations and climates will start to look very different from each other. So over thousands and millions of years, you can go from tiny **trap-door spiders** to hefty, desert-dwelling **tarantulas** and hairy-bodied **Arctic wolf spiders**. And this is not just how *spider* species adapt and change – it's how *all* species change. We call it **evolution by natural selection**.

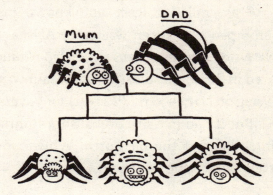

**Smart. So have any *other* cold-blooded things made homes in the Arctic? You know, besides spiders?**

As a matter of fact, yes. Believe it or not there are Arctic **mosquitos**, Arctic **bumblebees**, even Arctic **butterflies**! Each has its own adaptations to living in extreme cold. **Arctic bumblebees**, for example, use their larger wing muscles to shiver and generate heat. **Arctic white butterflies** weave an ice-proof chrysalis to protect them through the coldest months. And **Arctic nose bot flies** lay their eggs inside the warm noses of unfortunate caribou.

And though there are no Arctic reptiles **now**, there may have been **once**. Roughly **70 million years ago**, back when the Arctic wasn't quite as chilly, at least one known prehistoric reptile stomped the frozen wastes of Alaska – a pint-sized relative of *Tyrannosaurus rex*, called *Nanuqsaurus*. Discovered in 2014, this dwarf tyrannosaur was roughly half the size of *T. rex* – 6 m (20 feet) long, versus 12 m (40 feet). But it had massive eyeballs for hunting in the low, wintry light of the far north. Which would have made it a spooky thing to behold.

**A tiny Arctic tyrannosaurus?! That's like the coolest thing I've heard this year!**

*Cool*est. Ha. I see what you did there.

**What? Oh, yeah. Hahaha.**

# QUICK ONES –
# SNAKES AND SPIDERS

**How many of the world's snakes and spiders are venomous?**

There are about **3,000** species of **snake** in the world, but only **600** are venomous. Of these, only **200** have a powerful enough venom to kill or seriously injure a human. These include the Australian **brown snake**, the African **black mamba**, and the Indian **krait**.

Put another way, only **7%** (or 1 in 14) snake species are dangerous, and the other **93%** (13 out of 14 species) are **harmless**.

As for **spiders**, there are over **43,000** species worldwide, and most of them have some kind of venom.

But less than 1% of these (1 in 100) are dangerous to humans, and only **30** (**1 in 1,400**) spider species are considered deadly to humans. These include certain types of **widow**, **recluse**, and **funnel-web** spider. Even if you *are* bitten by one of these bad boys, death by spider bite is now vanishingly rare, thanks to modern **antivenin** (a.k.a. **anti-venom**) drugs.

## Why do all the venomous things live in Australia?

Actually, they don't. Australia only has **66** venomous animal species total, compared to **79** in Brazil, and **80** in Mexico. But it is home to **20** out of the **25 most venomous snakes** in the world, including the most venomous – the **inland taipan** (a.k.a. **fierce snake**).

Snakes first evolved over **140 million years ago**, when **dinosaurs** still roamed the Earth, and Africa, Australia, Antarctica, and South America were mostly still joined together in a **single, giant landmass.** It is likely that the snakes that first settled in Australia over 100 million years ago were venomous. So when the Australian, American, and African continents split apart, theses founding species became marooned and developed ever-more toxic venoms over time.

We don't know for sure why they became *so* toxic. But it could be because much of Australia is covered in desert or sparse scrubland (the famous Australian 'bush'), where prey is hard to find, and allowing even one animal to struggle free might mean starving to death. Strong venom allows smaller snakes and spiders to overcome larger prey without struggle. It could also be that native animals in Australia became resistant to snake and spider bites, driving the evolution of ever-more-powerful venoms in a kind of arms race.

In any case – if you see a snake in Australia, **leave it alone**. Snakes very rarely attack unprovoked, and most deadly bites are acts of serpentine self-defence.

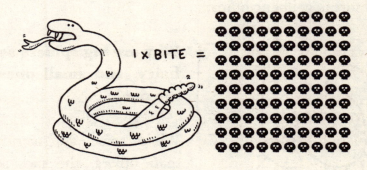

**Could a snake swallow a person?**

Put simply – yes. But only a few kinds of snake could do it, and it almost never happens.

The only snakes capable of swallowing a person are giant **constrictors**, like **pythons** and **boas**, which wrap around their prey and strangle them to death before swallowing. These snakes have special adaptations for swallowing large animals whole, including jaws that detach (or dislocate) to slip over their prey, and stomachs that stretch to fit an entire animal body.

**Burmese pythons** (6 m long) and **African rock pythons** (7.5 m long) prey on pigs, dogs, and goats – but not people. **Reticulated pythons** (6 m long) and **green anacondas** (up to 10 m long) have been known to swallow pigs, deer, caimans (a type of alligator), and – very occasionally – people. Thankfully, both these species are rather shy, move pretty slowly, and rarely resort to gobbling humans.

### Why are big spiders so hairy, and small ones are not?

While some are hairier than others, the fact is *all* spiders are hairy. Put *any* spider under the microscope and you'll see hairs on its legs and body. These hairs serve a wide range of purposes.

The microscopic hairs on spiders' **feet** (called **scopular hairs**) give them better grip for climbing.

More fine hairs on the legs and body help the spiders to smell, taste, and hear – sensing chemicals and vibrations in the air (or, for web-building spiders, in their webs). In some species, dense hairs on their bodies **trap air** around the spiders, to help prevent them from drowning. And famously hairy **tarantulas** have special stinging hairs – called **urticating hairs** – which they release in a cloud to deter attackers, stinging their eyes and faces. In short, spiders are both hairy and *cool*.

## Do spiders have noses?

No, they do not. While mammals use noses for breathing and smelling, spiders smell with hairs on their legs and feet (see previous question), and breathe through a network of tiny tubes called **tracheae** (pronounced 'track-ii-ay'). Tracheae are found in most **spiders**, **insects**, and other **arthropods.** They help funnel oxygen from the air through the animal's chunky **exoskeleton** and into its muscles and tissues. Most spiders (and scorpions) have **book lungs** – special blood-filled plates over which air circulates, moving oxygen into the blood. Some spiders have *both* tracheae *and* book lungs, while others have one or the other. But alas – none of them have noses.

# EARTH, SPACE, AND ALIENS

# WHY IS THE EARTH SHAPED LIKE A BALL?

Most planets – including ours – begin life as huge, spinning *discs*. But over time, gravity causes that disc to squash and clump together, making a big, rocky 'bubble' in space.

## Wait – planets start off as discs?

Yup. Massive discs of dust and gas, encircling newly formed stars in baby solar systems. Astronomers call these **accretion discs**. Depending on how big the star

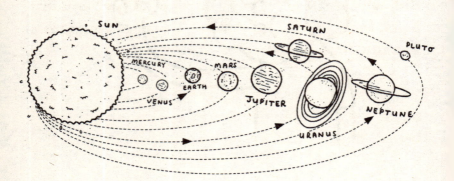

is – and how strong its gravity is – the disc might separate into one or more rocky **rings**. These would look much like the rings of ice and rock that currently surround Saturn and other gas giant planets in our own solar system. Only much bigger, and centered on the Sun rather than a planet. The Jovian asteroid belt – between Mars and Jupiter – is the result of this process in our own solar system.

In some accretion discs, small whirls of dust (called eddies) might condense into spinning **planetesimals** or **protoplanets** – clumps of gas, dust, and rock a mile (1.5 km) or more across. Over millions of years, these baby planets might smash together and split apart, or clump together via their shared gravity. Depending on how much material they have to work with, these clumps might become huge, ball-shaped planets like Earth, Mars, and Venus, or max out as smaller, lumpier protoplanets or dwarf planets.

**But why do they always end up as big, round *balls*, instead of . . . I dunno . . . egg-shaped, or banana-shaped planets?**

Good question. Ask the average person that, and they might say something like 'because round things spin better'. But this doesn't quite make sense. The Earth *does* spin, of course. And round things *do* spin well. But saying the Earth is round *because* it spins is like saying 'hands are flat so they can hold smartphones'.

Besides that, discs and cylinders spin just fine, don't they? So why are planets big gas-balls and rock-balls, rather than discs, tubes, or cylinders?

The real reason has less to do with spin, and more to do with **gravity**.

When most people hear the word gravity, they think of a force which pulls things down. This makes sense. After all, ideas about what gravity is and what gravity does have changed quite a bit over the last 500 years.

In the late 1500s, the Italian astronomer and scientist **Galileo Galilei** described gravity as **a force of attraction between an object and the ground**.

In the 1600s, British smarty-pants (and incidentally, inventor of the cat flap) **Sir Isaac Newton** altered this view, explaining that gravity was a **force of attraction between any two objects with mass**. It just so happens that for us, the Earth is the most massive object around. So all objects on its surface – including people, oceans and falling apples – are constantly being pulled towards its centre.

Then in the early 1900s, troll-haired Swiss scientist **Albert Einstein** changed our view of gravity once *again*. According to Einstein, gravity is actually **a warping**

**of four-dimensional spacetime around massive objects** which causes them **to 'fall' or 'roll' towards each other.**

## Errr . . . what?

If you have trouble getting your head around that, then join the club. It's hard for us to imagine any more than three dimensions, as that's all our eyes and brains are wired to perceive. Think of it this way – a planet floating in spacetime is like a **heavy basketball** placed on a big sheet. The weight of the ball dents (or **warps**) the fabric of spacetime around it, causing any and all weighty objects close enough to the 'dent' to roll into it.

Eventually, all such objects will smack into the ball in the middle. That is, unless their inward fall is balanced out by another, outward, force. That's where spin comes in. Moons fail to crash into planets – and planets into their parent stars – because they're formed from large, spinning discs. This spin flings moons and planets outwards, balancing out the inward pull of gravity and holding them (at least for a time), in a stable orbit.

## Okay, but I still don't get why that makes planets into balls or spheres.

That's all down to the planet's *own* gravity, pulling on the planet itself.

While it's difficult for us to imagine solid rock and metal 'flowing', over very long periods of time that's exactly what they do. Over millions of years, the rocky mass of a planet actually acts like a liquid. So when the gravitational field of a newly formed planet tries to pull everything towards its centre of mass – which is the middle of the 'dent' its mass creates in space – the rock and metal flow towards the planet's centre, making a sphere.

In reality, planets rarely form *perfect* spheres. For starters, any planet with a good amount of rotation or spin will tend to bulge outward in the middle, like a middle-aged dad. This makes the planet slightly squashed (or **oblate**)*.

If a newly formed planetoid isn't big enough (i.e. lacks enough mass), then its gravitational field won't be strong enough to pull it into a perfectly spherical shape. For this reason, many asteroids, moons and dwarf

* This is actually the case for the Earth. It's *almost* a perfect sphere, but not quite. It's actually a little wider across the equator than it is from pole to pole.

planets end up with **elongated**, **egg-like**, or **lumpy**, **irregular shapes**.

**Seriously? There are egg-shaped moons and dwarf planets up there? Hahahaha! Which ones?**

The two moons of Mars – **Phobos** and **Deimos** – are both shaped like lumpy potatoes, rather than spheres. As are several of Saturn's smaller moons, like **Hyperion**, **Pandora** and **Prometheus**. And at least one known dwarf planet – called **Haumea** – is egg-shaped, and tumbles clumsily through space.

**Hahahaha. Cool!**

Who knows – maybe one day we'll land on an egg-shaped world, build a colony, and raise chickens on its surface.

**I'd call it *Eggthon*. No wait – *Nuggetz*.**

Good choice. Very . . . majestic.

# EGG WORLDS
# (AND OTHER CRAZY PLANETS)

### Haumea – the Egg World

Haumea is an egg-shaped dwarf planet in our own solar system, orbiting beyond Neptune. It is about one third the size of Pluto. Named after a Hawaiian goddess of fertility, it has two moons (Hi'aka and Namaka), a ring system, and a thick coat of ice upon its rocky surface. It rotates so fast that one day on Haumea lasts just 3 hours and 54 minutes.

### Gliese – World of Fire and Ice

Gliese 581c is an exoplanet 120 trillion miles (192 trillion km) away, which orbits its parent star less than one tenth the distance that the Earth orbits the Sun.

One side of its surface always faces its star, while the other always faces away. So if you stood on one side it would melt you alive, and on the other you would freeze solid. Its not clear if anything lives there, but we sent it a radio signal, just in case.

## Cancri – the Diamond Planet
55 Cancri E is about 40 light-years from Earth, is about twice the size of our planet, and is thought to be largely made of carbon. It has a surface temperature of over 2400°C (4400°F). This, together with its enormous atmospheric pressure, could create diamonds at its surface. The entire planet might be covered with them.

## Ogle – Snowball Planet
Ogle-2005-Blg-390lb is about 20,000 light-years from us. It orbits a small red dwarf star, and at such a distance that it barely gets any heat from it. For this reason, it is one of the coldest planets yet discovered, with a surface temperature of -220°C (-364°F).

## Tres – the Puffy Planet
TrES-4b is an enormous exoplanet around 1,400 light-years away. Almost twice the size of Jupiter, TrES-4b is both extremely hot and extremely light and puffy. It has about the same density as a cork in a bottle.

# IF THE EARTH HAS EARTHQUAKES, DOES THE MOON HAVE MOONQUAKES?

At least one or two moons in our solar system – including our own – do experience earthquakes. Or rather, moonquakes.

## Let's start with earthquakes. Why do we get them at all?

Earthquakes have been around since the formation of the planet, over 4.5 billion years ago. But until the nineteenth century, no one had a decent (or rather correct) explanation for why they happened.

In ancient Greece and Rome, people believed they were the work of a fire god who lived beneath the earth. The Greeks called him **Hephaestus**, while the Romans knew him as **Vulcan**. According to legend,

Vulcan was the blacksmith to the gods, and caused earthquakes with every beat of his hammer, along with volcanic eruptions from the chimneys of his forge.

The Japanese – no strangers to a tremor or two – had another explanation. Earthquakes, they said, were caused by the stirrings of an **enormous catfish** who lived beneath the island.

# A giant underground catfish? Riiiiight.

To be fair, neither the ancient Greeks nor the ancient Japanese had science to tell them otherwise. By the 1800s, the science of **geology** had arrived. And with it, some more logical ideas about what might be going on below the Earth's surface.

In 1911, German scientist **Alfred Lothar Wegener** noticed that the coastal outlines of western Africa and eastern South America would actually **fit together** quite nicely, if you looked at them like pieces of a jigsaw puzzle. From this, he guessed (quite correctly) that they had **once been part of the same, huge supercontinent**. One had split apart, way back in the Earth's history, leaving the continents to drift apart over time. He called this idea the **theory of continental drift**.

In 1962, geologist and US Navy captain **Harry Hammond Hess** (almost certainly known to his friends as 'Triple H') came up with his **theory of sea-floor spreading**.

This explained how **magma** bubbled up from mid-ocean **ridges**, creating new **sea-floor** on either side, which would then spread across the sea-bed and eventually be sucked back into the Earth at deep ocean **trenches** thousands of miles away.

Then in 1967, cunning British geoscientist **Dan McKenzie** took both these ideas and fused them into one, big theory of geological everything – **the theory of plate tectonics**.

This theory explained that Hess's sea-floor spreading was the **cause of** Wegener's **continental drift**. Helpfully, plate tectonics also explained why earthquakes, volcanic eruptions, and all sorts of other geological phenomena happen.

**So why *do* they happen?**

According to the theory of plate tectonics, the **continents** actually sit on top of a series of **enormous crusty plates**, which in turn surf upon **a sea of molten rock** (or **magma**) below. Fresh magma bubbles up at mid-ocean ridges, creating new crust and spreading the plates apart. The continents ride along on top of the plates like luggage on a conveyer belt.

Where the plates meet, they either slip under and over each other – the edges buckling upwards to form **mountain ranges**, or crashing and grinding together.

**Wait – so mountains start off really small, then grow bigger and bigger as the land smashes together and folds up?**

Exactly. In fact, that is how pretty much all of the world's mountain ranges – the Alps, the Andes, and the Himalayas – were formed.

The Himalayas, for example, began forming after the plate bearing **India** (or rather, the landmass we now recognize as India) drifted northwards across the equator and smashed into the **Eurasian plate** (currently holding up Russia, Europe, and most of Asia).

Where the two landmasses met, the Indian plate **slipped under** the Eurasian plate, buckling and lifting the land to form the Tibetan Plateau, and forming a range of mountains over **2,400 km (1,500 miles) long**.

The Himalayan range includes over **50 mountains over 7,000 m (23,000 feet) high** – including the famous **Mount Everest (8,848 m or 29,029 feet)**. The range stretches from Afghanistan and Pakistan in the west all the way to northern Myanmar in the east. It separates northern India from southern China, with three countries – **Nepal**, **Tibet**, and **Bhutan** – nestled in between, atop the range itself.

**Whoa! India smashed into China?! When did that happen?**

About 50 million years ago, a good while *after* the K–T extinction event (66 million years ago) that killed off most of the dinosaurs. In other words, **when dinosaurs walked the Earth, the Himalayas had not even formed yet**. Which means Mount Everest is **younger** than *Tyrannosaurus rex*.

**Mind . . . blown.**

Right? Geology is *awesome*.

**So where do the earthquakes come in?**

That's easy – **wherever tectonic plates crash and grind together, you get earthquakes.** This is because the rough edges of each plate are continually getting stuck, and pressure builds as they keep trying to move past each other. Eventually, though, something has to give. So when the plates slip again, the pressure is released with a powerful juddering motion – otherwise known as an **earthquake**.

For this reason, most earthquakes happen **at or near plate boundaries**, like the one that runs down the west coast of the USA, and the one that runs right along the middle of Japan. **Volcanoes** and **volcanic activity** are also common along plate boundaries, as magma bubbles up between the plates as they slip and crumble.

In fact, the outer edges of the same, enormous Pacific Plate form a huge ring – known as the **Ring of Fire** – that traces the length of Japan, the Philippines, New Zealand and the entire west coast of the Americas. This is why we see so many earthquakes in these regions, and why volcanoes are common in these places, too.

RING OF FIRE

## Coooool. So does this all happen on the Moon and other planets, too?

Astronomers have known about moonquakes since 1972, when astronauts from the **Apollo 17** mission felt them while bouncing around on the Moon's surface. Since then, robot probes and orbiters have observed over 450 tremors on Mars, and at least one tremor on Mercury. So you can go ahead and add **Marsquakes** and **Mercuryquakes** to your new list of words. Venus very likely has **Venusquakes**, also – though the scorching temperatures and pressures of its atmosphere makes them hard to detect, and has thus far destroyed every probe we have sent down to its surface.

Moonquakes, Marsquakes, and Mercuryquakes seem to be a little different from earthquakes. The Moon seems to have just one tectonic plate, which cracks and shudders in response to meteorite impacts. It also expands and contracts as the Moon spins in and out of direct sunlight. So while earthquakes typically only last a minute or so, Moonquakes can last for several hours.

Until recently, we assumed Mars was totally silent and still. But scientists now think Mars's crust may be cracked into many plates or fragments, creating weak, frequent Marsquakes that go on for 30 minutes or more.

Mercuryquakes are still something of a mystery. But they may be related to the fact that Mercury is slowly shrinking – creating cracks and folds in its shell-like surface.

## What about volcanoes? Have we found those on other moons and planets, too?

Yup – we certainly have. **Venus** has more volcanoes than any other planet in the solar system (and some of them are likely still active!). **Jupiter** has a hellish, foul-smelling volcanic moon called **Io** (pronounced 'eye-o'), and **Saturn** has an ice-moon called **Encedalus,** which is home to strange **cryo-volcanoes** that spew ice thousands of miles out into space.

## What about Uranusquakes?

As far as we know, Uranus, Neptune and the other gas giant planets *can't* really have earthquakes, as they have no solid crust or plates to grind together.

**That's not true. You can get Uranusquakes sometimes.**

What? When?

**When you eat too many baked beans!**

Grrrrr . . .

**Bwahahahahahahaha!**

# EARTHQUAKES, MOONQUAKES, AND MARSQUAKES

There's a whole lotta shakin' goin' on.

The Earth's surface is broken into **20 constantly moving tectonic plates**, which create earthquakes as they slide and grind against each other. The two largest of these are the **Pacific** and **Antarctic** plates.

Almost **80% of earthquakes** happen around the rim of the Pacific Plate.

**Moonquakes** were first discovered by NASA astronauts and scientists in the 1970s. Moonquakes tend to be much weaker than earthquakes, but can last for an entire afternoon.

**Marsquakes** were thought to be very rare (as in once every million years) until the InSight Mars Lander detected four of them between March and April 2019. We have no clear idea what might be causing them.

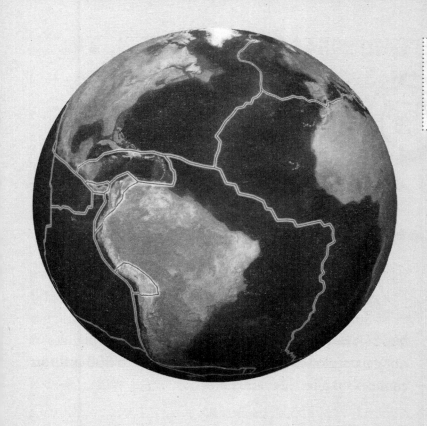

# WHY IS EARTH THE ONLY PLANET WITH LIFE ON IT?

Earth is the only planet that we know **for sure** has life. But that doesn't mean life isn't still lurking elsewhere, waiting to be discovered. It's a big, big universe, and the number of habitable planets in our galaxy alone could mean there are up to **500 million** chances for alien life out there!

**So could there be aliens right here in our solar system? Like on Mars or Venus?**

As far as we know – and after 50 years of looking – there is no complex, alien life on Mars or Venus right now. It is *possible* that some super-tough, single-celled bacterial life might still be lurking on or below the surface of those planets (more on that later). But we are pretty certain that Earth is the only planet in the solar system on which large, complex life forms like plants and animals have made a home. And it is possible we Earthlings are the only kind of life at all, anywhere in the solar system.

**But how do we know that for sure?**

Well, we don't. But based on everything we've learned to date, it's hard to see how life (as we know it) could develop and survive on any of the other planets.

A big part of this is down to **temperatures**. Almost all living creatures have trouble staying alive at temperatures **above 50°C (113°F)**, or **below -50°C**

**(-60ºF)**. Some bacteria found in volcanic springs and vents can survive temperatures up to **121ºC (250ºF)**. Others have been found frozen and dormant – but still alive – inside the ice sheets of the Antarctic. But for the most part, **life doesn't like extreme heat or cold**. And this is exactly what you find on the other seven planets.

The Earth sits at a comfortable distance from the Sun, within a region that astrobiologists call the **Goldilocks Zone**. Here, it's neither too hot, nor too cold. It's just right. Just like the porridge stolen by the selfish, prissy girl in the fairy tale*.

...................................................................................................................
* Stolen from a *baby bear*, no less. What a heartless thief!

On **Venus** – the next planet closest to the Sun after ours – surface temperatures can top **480°C (900°F)**. On **Mars**, one planet further away from the Sun than Earth, the average temperature is **-55°C (-67°F)**, and may drop as low as **-143°C (-225°F)** at the poles. So you wouldn't want to take a holiday on either one.

So being in the Goldilocks Zone keeps Earth's temperatures within a comfortable (or at least survivable) range for life. But sadly, none of the other planets lie within that zone.

**Yeah, but if all you need for alien life is the right *temperature*, then couldn't there be loads of other planets with aliens on them? Maybe not *here*, but somewhere else in the galaxy?**

There certainly could be. Astronomers think there are over **50 billion** planets in the Milky Way – the medium-sized, spiral galaxy we happen to live in. More than **500 million** of those planets lie within the Goldilocks Zone of their parent stars. Meaning any one of them could be the right temperature to allow life. But for life to develop, you need more than a comfortable climate. Think about it – what else do all living things need?

**Errr . . . water?**

Very good – right you are! All (and I mean *all*) known forms of life need liquid water to survive. The bodies of bacteria, plants and animals (including humans) are mostly made of water – up to **80**% water in many species. Liquid water provides a medium – or a place – in which the biomolecules that make life possible can interact. Without water, you can't even build a strand of DNA, let alone a protein, a shell, a bone, or a brain.

As far as we know, Earth is the only planet in the solar system with ample quantities of liquid water. On planets closer to the Sun, water simply boils off into space. Further from the Sun, all you're likely to find is ice*. Neither state is particularly helpful for living things. Hence, the presence of liquid water on Earth goes a long way towards explaining why we're (probably) all alone in the solar system.

**What if some planet got its water another way? Like if a watery planet or comet crashed into another one, and kind of *gave* it its water?**

That could actually happen. In fact, astronomers think that may be how our planet got its water. Many

---

* We recently discovered massive **lakes** of water beneath the carbon dioxide ice caps of Mars. But all of that water now exists as **ice** – which cannot support life as liquid lakes and oceans do.

**asteroids** and **protoplanets** – such as the asteroid **Vesta**, in the asteroid belt beyond Mars – contain water with chemical signatures very similar to that of Earth water. Which means it is very likely that water was **delivered** to us by icy asteroids and comets bombarding the surface of the young Earth, billions of years ago.

But in order to **keep** its life-friendly liquid water, a planet still has to be in that Goldilocks Zone where it **won't freeze or boil off**. Venus very likely had water once, but all its water has long since evaporated. Mars may also have had liquid water during its early formation, when its core and surface was much warmer. But now only ice remains.

**Okay – so as long as a planet has water, and sits in the Goldilocks Zone, then its good for cooking up some aliens?**

Not necessarily. As a home for life, the Earth has a few more things going for it, too.

It has a powerful **magnetic field**, which helpfully deflects and absorbs dangerous **radiation** originating from the Sun and other cosmic sources.

It has an **oxygen-rich atmosphere** – largely built by early forms of life – which has allowed larger, more complex forms of life to develop.

And it has an **asteroid shield,** in the form of our solar system's 'big daddy', **Jupiter**. With its immense mass and gravitational field, Jupiter deflects and absorbs many large asteroids and comets that would otherwise strike our planet. In doing so, Jupiter saves us from planet-killing rock-bombs that would wipe out life on Earth with annoying regularity.

Granted, Jupiter doesn't catch them *all*. Just ask the dinosaurs (oh, wait – you can't). But without it, life on Earth probably wouldn't have got very far.

**Okay, fine. So how many planets in our galaxy have all those things? Like, all the things you need for life to evolve and grow?**

Well, if you take all the known planets in Goldilocks Zones (maybe 500 million), then if even 1 in 1,000 of them have all these features, that would leave **half a million** planets capable of supporting some sort of alien life. What that life might actually look like is anybody's guess.

Some of those habitable planets are so-called **'super-Earths'** – and *way* bigger than ours. This would mean much stronger gravity, and much stronger muscles and limbs required for crawling, oozing, or scuttling around. Here, you might get some sort of giant worm, or a massive land-crab with super-thick shells and legs. But probably nothing that leaps or flies.

Other planets might **spin faster or slower** than ours, giving longer or shorter day/night cycles, and creating extremes of hot and cold. Some planets might have slowed their spin so much that they are effectively 'locked' with one side facing their parent star – so that it's always roasting hot on one side of the planet, and freezing cold on the other. You might imagine a planet with strange, desert-dwelling creatures on one side, and furry snow-beasts on the other.

**Now that would be cool. So what about intelligent life? Something more like us?**

We haven't seen any evidence of intelligent aliens or alien civilizations elsewhere in our galaxy yet. If they were up there, you might think we would have detected radio waves or other signals from the stars and systems they live in. Then again, maybe they're just too far away, or we haven't looked in the right place yet. Maybe alien civilizations are developing elsewhere, but they're still in the prehistoric or medieval stage – building pyramids or castles, but not towns and cities just yet. It took life on Earth about 4.5 billion years to get from squidging around in the oceans to building skyscrapers, rockets, and radio telescopes.

One astronomer recently estimated all the habitable planets and systems in the galaxy, subtracted all the ones less than 4.5 billion years old, and came up with a number for how many intelligent alien civilizations we should expect to find.

**So how many does he reckon?**

At least 36.

**Hahaha. Cool!**

Right or wrong, with
as many habitable planets
as there are, it's certainly
possible that intelligent life
is out there somewhere.
Who knows – maybe *Star
Wars* isn't so far from
the truth. Let's just
hope they're
friendly . . .

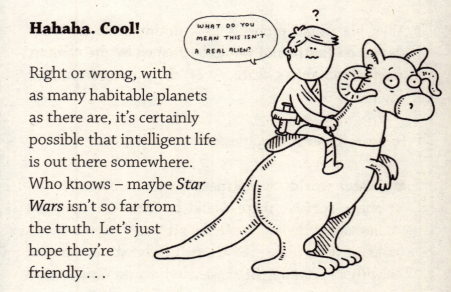

WHAT DO YOU MEAN THIS ISN'T A REAL ALIEN?

# WHAT MIGHT ALIENS LOOK LIKE?

Alien life would probably look nothing like anything we see on Earth, and would be shaped by the climate, gravity and other features of their extra-terrestrial environment.

Here are a few possibilities:

● **Water world** – on planets where oceans cover the entire surface, there would be little use for solid limbs and skeletons. Aliens on water worlds would likely look more like starfish, jellyfish, octopuses, with a sprinkling of sharks and manta rays. Maybe some of them might take to the air, evolving into strange alien fish-birds.

- **Subsurface ocean world** – many moons and exoplanets have frozen surfaces that could be hiding liquid oceans beneath, warmed by the molten core of the world. Here, you might find things similar to our deep-sea fish and crustaceans – lobsters, tube worms, corals. With no light from the surface, they might also have no eyes, and see-through bodies!

- **Super-Earth** – several 'super-Earths' (planets several times larger than our own) have been found in other solar systems. These planets would likely have much stronger gravitational fields, forcing aliens there to evolve thicker muscles, skeletons or exoskeletons to help them move around. These might look more like thick-legged dinosaurs or giant land crabs than humans.

# WHY DOES THE MOON CHANGE SHAPE?

Because the Moon orbits (or circles) the Earth roughly once every 29.5 days, casting shadows on the Moon's surface that shift and change shape throughout the lunar month. These moon-shapes (or phases) go through a repeating pattern, based on where the Moon is in its Earth-centred orbit.

**So the Moon doesn't really change shape? It just seems to?**

Right. The Moon itself never changes. Only the patterns of light and shadow on its surface.

**So what shape is it really?**

The shape it appears to be at full moon – a near-perfect sphere. Like all moons, it's a big ball of rock in space –

smaller than a planet, but larger than an asteroid, and locked into a circular orbit by the gravitational pull of its parent planet, the Earth*.

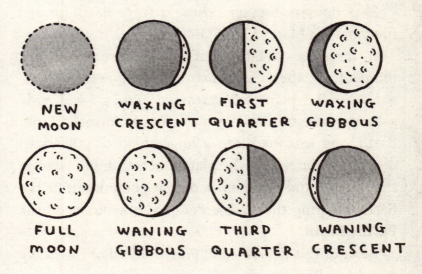

NEW MOON    WAXING CRESCENT    FIRST QUARTER    WAXING GIBBOUS

FULL MOON    WANING GIBBOUS    THIRD QUARTER    WANING CRESCENT

**How did the Moon even get up there? Where did it come from?**

That's a very good question. Every culture has its own story about where the Sun, Moon, and stars came from. The ancient Egyptians believed the Moon was a god called **Khonsu** – the son of the sun god and earth god.

.................................................................................

* Or rather, locked into the combined pull of the two objects *on each other*. The Moon's gravity pulls on the Earth, too, creating, among other things, our daily ocean tides.

The ancient Maya believed the Moon was a goddess (first known as **Selene**, later **Artemis**) and wife of the sun god (**Helios** or **Apollo**).

Astronomers, though, believe that the Earth formed first, and the Moon a little later.

As far as we can tell, about 4.5 billion years ago, in a moment of spectacular astronomical awesomeness, a Mars-sized planetoid screamed through the early solar system, smashed into the newly formed planet Earth, and exploded into a huge cloud of pulverized dust, rock and metal. The planetoid was annihilated in the impact, and also blew a massive chunk out of the Earth, creating the sizable dent we now know as the **Pacific Basin**.

Most of this debris – and practically all of the heavy metals – fell back to the Earth.

But some stayed in orbit, forming a temporary ring around the planet, similar to the ones we still see around **Saturn** and **Uranus**. Over a few million years, though, the larger rocks in the ring were pulled together by their own gravity, and formed the big, rocky ball we know as the Moon.

This is called the **giant impactor theory**, and it neatly explains why moon rocks look like they do (like earth rocks, minus the heavy metals), how the Pacific Basin formed, and why the Earth spins faster than you would expect it to (its rotation sped up when the planetoid bomb cannoned into it like a cosmic cue-ball).

It is also one of the most awesome things you will ever hear. Fact.

**Yeah, that *is* pretty awesome. Okay – so if the shape is caused by sunlight and shadows, then where is the Sun when it's a full moon?**

At any given time, **half** the Moon's surface is being struck by sunlight. Depending on where we are relative to the Moon, we may get to see the **whole 'lit' side**, **none** of it, **half** of it, or **somewhere in between**. This creates the various visible shapes or **phases of the Moon**.

At **full moon**, the Moon has moved to the far side of Earth, on the opposite side to the Sun. Sunlight strikes the entire, Earth-facing side of the Moon, and we see it as a full, bright circle or disc.

At **new moon** (about 15 days later) the Moon has moved to the other side – between the Sun and the Earth. Now the Moon's backside (as it were) is being lit up by the Sun, while its entire Earth-facing side lies in shadow. So to us, the Moon seems to vanish against the dark background of space.

## What about the bits in between?

Well, at the **first quarter** phase, the Moon lies to the **side** of the Earth. If you looked down on the whole system from above, the line between the Earth and Moon would form a **90-degree angle** between the Sun and the Earth. Viewed from above, the **sun-facing side** would be the **left** side. But from Earth, the sun-facing side is on the **right**. So at first quarter, the Moon appears half-full – the **right side bright**, the **left side dark**.

Between the **new moon** and **first quarter** phases, the Moon is moving from **back-lit** to **half-lit**. So for a day or so after new moon, we see only a thin **crescent** of light reflecting from its right-hand edge. Over the course of a week, this crescent **widens** to cover half the Moon's surface.

## So what comes after that?

A week later, the Moon has circled to the **far** side of the Earth, and appears **full**. A week after *that*, it's at **third quarter**, on the **opposite** side than it was at **first quarter**. Now the sun-facing half of the Moon (as seen from Earth) is on the **left**, while the **right** side lies in shadow.

In the week between **third quarter** and **new moon**, the Moon is shifting from **half-lit** to **backlit**. So the lit-up portion of its surface gradually shrinks – from a semicircle to a thin crescent on the Moon's **left-hand** edge.

Between **first quarter** and **full moon**, the Moon is circling from a **half-lit** to a **fully lit** position, so light covers between 50% and 100% of its visible surface. Between full moon and third quarter, the reverse happens – the lit-up portion decreases from 100% to 50%. We call these the **gibbous phases** of the Moon. This is when the Moon looks **podgy, but not quite full**.

This same sequence of shape-changes happens every month – progressing through **new moon, crescent, first quarter, gibbous, full, gibbous, third quarter, crescent**, and back around again.

Between new moon and full moon, we say the Moon is **waxing**; between full moon and new moon, we say it's **waning**. Got it?

**I think so. So . . . what would happen if the Moon *didn't* orbit around the Earth? Would it just stay the same shape?**

In theory, yes. If the Moon became somehow locked in place between the Sun and Earth, and *stayed* in

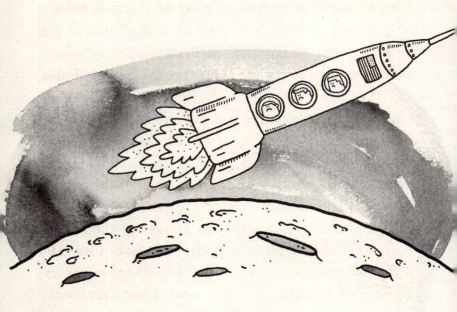

that position as the whole Earth-Moon system orbited around the Sun, then it would remain a new moon all year round. If it stopped on the far side of the Earth, creating a line from Sun to Earth to Moon, it would be **full** all year round (or possibly in a year-round lunar eclipse).

In reality, the Moon cannot just stop its orbit. And you really wouldn't *want* it to.

### Why's that?

Because if the Moon even *slowed* its circular orbit – let alone *stopped* it – it would be pulled right into the Earth at 25,000 mph, smashing the Earth to bits, and turning it into a ball of molten rock with no oceans, no atmosphere, and no life.

**Oh. Let's not do *that*, then.
Keep going, Moon!**

# MOON FACTS

The Moon: no cheese up there, sorry!

● The **Moon is made of the same stuff as the Earth** – mostly **iron**, **silicon**, **magnesium**, and various **oxides** of those metals.

● The Moon has about **one sixth** the gravitational pull of the Earth, meaning you could jump between **3 and 15 metres** on the Moon – depending on how good you are at jumping.

● The Moon **always shows us the same side** (or face), as it circles us. This means it also has a **dark side** that only a handful of astronauts have ever seen (cue Darth Vader breathing).

● To date, humans have landed on the Moon just **six** times. All of these landing missions took place between **1969 and 1972**, and all of them were American (NASA) missions.

WHOOSH!

● At least **six** countries are planning to land on the Moon between 2020 and 2030. These include China, Russia, India, Japan, South Korea, and the USA (again).

# TRY IT YOURSELF: MAKE YOUR OWN MOON CHART

- Using the bottom of a small cup, trace 8 identical circles on a piece of black construction paper.

- Cut out each circle and glue them horizontally onto a long piece of blue paper.

- With white paint or chalk, colour in each moon phase from new moon to waning crescent, and label all eight moon phases.

- Use your moon phases chart to observe the moon each evening for a month, noting which phase the moon is in.

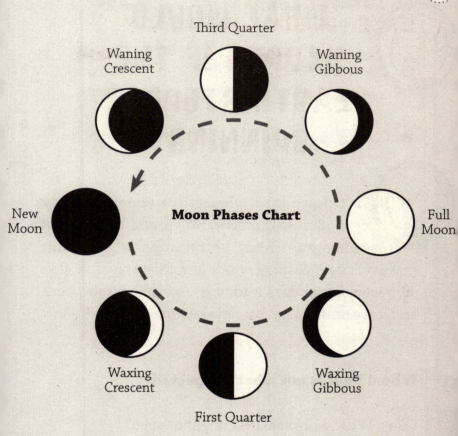

**Moon Phases Chart**

Third Quarter

Waning Crescent

Waning Gibbous

New Moon

Full Moon

Waxing Crescent

Waxing Gibbous

First Quarter

# WHAT WOULD HAPPEN IF THE EARTH STOPPED SPINNING?

That depends on whether it stopped suddenly, or if it slowed down and ground to a halt. A sudden stop would be catastrophic – creating massive, city-smashing winds and tidal waves. A slow stop would turn days into years, boil the atmosphere, and leave nothing but bacteria behind!

**Whoa! That is *not* what I expected.**

Okay. What did you expect might happen?

**Well, I thought it might mess with night and day a bit. I mean, doesn't the spin make night and day happen?**

You're right – it does. The Earth spins (or **rotates**) on its axis roughly once every 24 hours. This creates our regular cycles of day and night, as our villages, towns, countries, and continents spin in and out of the sunshine.

From our point of view on the ground, the Sun seems to arc across the sky – **rising** in the east every morning, and **setting** in the west every night. The **Moon** – whether we see it by day or by night – follows the same pattern, arcing across the sky from east to west. Even the **stars** rise and set this way – though it can be hard to notice, unless you track a specific star or constellation all night.

In reality, the Sun, Moon, and stars are not really moving this way at all. It is *us* that is moving. The little patch of ground upon which we live, work, and gaze up at the sky is spinning in space, bringing the Sun, Moon, and stars in

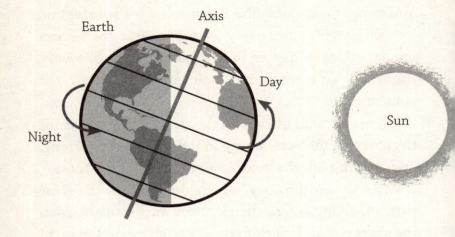

Earth

Axis

Day

Night

Sun

and out of view, and making it look like they're racing past (or over) us in the opposite direction.

At any given time, half the Earth is bathed in sunlight, and half the Earth lies in shadow. Where there is light, it is daytime; where it is dark, it is night-time. As the Earth spins, the sunlit and shadowed parts of its surface are swapped. So that every 24 hours (23 hours, 56 minutes, and 4 seconds, to be precise), every spot on the Earth gets to experience one long period of light (day), and one long period of darkness (night).

*Within* that 24 hours, the length of each day and night shifts and changes through the seasons, as the Earth's **tilt** and **orbit around the Sun** keeps some parts of the world in sunlight for longer, and others longer in shadow. But the length of the whole day-plus-night cycle always remains the same, at roughly 24 hours.

Now if the Earth were to stop rotating, then these day-night cycles would stop. Half the planet would stay in sunlight, and the other half would remain in darkness.

**So it would be daytime forever in some places, and night-time forever in others?**

Not quite. Even if the Earth stopped **spinning**, it would still be **moving through space** – **circling** the Sun, and completing a full **orbit** once every 365 days. This would bring a given spot on the Earth in and out of shadow once per year – **creating six months of day, and six months of night**, everywhere on Earth. That would seriously mess with surface temperatures, weather patterns, plant and animal life cycles, all kinds of things.

**Okay – I get that. But what about all that other stuff? Why would stopping the spin all of a sudden be so bad?**

Well, for starters, the Earth isn't just spinning. It's spinning *really fast*. As in, over **1,670 kilometres (1,038 miles) per hour**, depending on how far from the equator you live.

Imagine being on a huge roundabout doing 1,000 mph, and someone hit the brakes, stopping it instantly. What would happen?

**Errr – you'd fly off it at 1,000 mph, and, *really* hurt yourself.**

Right. Now imagine you, your school, your house, your entire town is perched on the roundabout, too. When the roundabout stops, all *those* things come rolling and crashing into each other as well. Worse yet, even the **oceans** and **atmosphere** would slosh around the Earth – creating hurricane-force winds and massive tsunamis that wipe out most of the planet's surface. In short, it would *not* be a fun ride.

# But if you slowed it down gently, little-by-little?

Then you would fare a little better. At least at first.

If you somehow managed to slow the Earth's spin – dragging it to a halt over the course of several weeks or months – then you could avoid the sudden crash of wind and water. But with no spin at all, the Earth's oceans would no longer be evenly spread across its surface. Instead, they would shift north and south towards the poles (where the pull of gravity is strongest), creating two deep polar oceans and a huge belt of dry land around the Earth's middle. This would submerge the whole of Antarctica, along with everything north of Spain, Japan, and New York City.

The remaining, un-submerged parts – southern Europe, Asia, Africa, Australia and the Americas – would be joined together into a single, giant supercontinent. You could literally walk* right around the middle of the planet.

.......................................................................................

* More like trek and *climb* – since you'd have to cross a few undersea obstacles like the Mid-Atlantic Ridge (over 2,000 m high) and the Mariana Trench (over 10,000 m deep!).

**That doesn't sound so bad.**

Hold on – we're not done yet. With no spin, the Earth's liquid-iron **core** would also stop rotating. This core rotation creates and maintains the Earth's **magnetic field** – an invisible barrier that protects us from deadly solar and cosmic radiation. Without it, the Earth's surface would be bombarded with massive amounts of radiation, killing off plants and animals across the globe.

Even if we managed to survive *all that,* we would still be left with six months of daytime, six months of night-time – as we talked about earlier. You might think that would be like having six months of summer, followed by six months of winter. But you would be wrong. In fact, with slower rotation and circulation, the airy atmosphere surrounding the planet would steadily heat up to over **100°C (212°F)**, turning the whole planet into a giant oven.

**Yikes! So if you weren't crushed or drowned by a sudden stop, you'd be baked and frazzled by a slow one?**

Like a sad rasher of bacon, or a cookie left too long in the oven. But happily, the world keeps on turning, and short of a massive impact with another planet-sized object, there's no known force that could bring it to a halt. Let's all be grateful for that – today, and every day!

# QUICK ONES –
# COMETS AND ASTEROIDS

**What's the difference between a comet and an asteroid?**

Actually, not that much. Comets and asteroids are both lumps of rock, metal, and ice pulled into long orbits around the Sun by its powerful gravitational field. But comets tend to contain more ice than asteroids, with a core (or **nucleus**) of rock surrounded by a thick, icy crust. Far from the Sun, it looks pretty much like an asteroid. But as a comet nears the Sun, the evaporation of ice gives it a gassy shell (called a **coma**), and makes it look fuzzy or blurred when viewed from Earth. It also leaves behind a **tail** of trailing debris – which can stretch right across the night sky. So they definitely *look* cooler than asteroids.

## Where do asteroids come from?

Most are bits of rocky or metallic debris leftover from the formation of the solar system, billions of years ago. The bits that *didn't* get sucked into the mass of the central sun, and *didn't* clump together into planets, dwarf planets, and moons. Instead, they got pulled into orbit around their host star (i.e. the Sun), forming one wide, circular **asteroid belt** between Mars and Jupiter, and another one out beyond Neptune. When these get knocked out of orbit, they sometimes move into new paths around the sun – putting them on a collision course with a planet or moon.

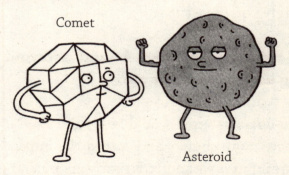

Comet

Asteroid

## Could you fly through an asteroid belt without crashing?

Yes, and very easily. The average distance between any two objects in the Jovian asteroid belt, for example, is about **a million miles**. That leaves plenty of room for your Starship, Battlestar, or Star Destroyer. No dodging, weaving, or pew-pew laser-beams required.

## How huge would an asteroid have to be to destroy the planet?

No asteroid or comet could ever destroy the planet itself – it's big enough to absorb any asteroid or comet impact and remain in one piece. But any asteroid larger than 1 km (0.6 miles) across would be enough to destroy 50-100% of life on the planet. This has happened before – at least twice. Happily, there don't seem to be any that big on the way . . .

## Could we stop an Earth-bound asteroid from hitting us by blowing it up?

Blowing up an asteroid would be a bad idea – it would just create more chunks and spread the impact over a wider area. But if we spotted it early enough, and could get to it quickly enough, we could maybe attach booster rockets or a solar sail to the asteroid in order to nudge it a few degrees off course, sending it safely wide of the Earth. Sounds crazy, but it could work!

# LIGHTNING, VOLCANOES, AND LIVING SYSTEMS

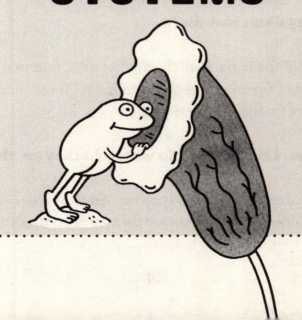

# WHERE DO ALL THE FIREFLIES GO IN THE WINTER?

Fireflies (or lightning bugs) buzz and flash their way through the summer, and seem to disappear by late autumn. But unlike birds, fireflies don't migrate to warmer places. Instead, they hide out for a couple of years before emerging in another, quite different form.

**So they don't just die?**

Not all of them, no. If *all* the fireflies died, that would be the end of the whole *species* wouldn't it? There would be no more fireflies the next year.

**Hmmm. I suppose so. So where do they go, then?**

Well, it depends how old they are. **Adult** fireflies spend the summer mating, then lay their eggs on the ground, and die soon afterwards. A few weeks later, those eggs hatch into baby fireflies, in the form of wriggling, caterpillar-like **larvae**. These larvae feed for the rest of the summer, then burrow into the ground* to hide out – or **hibernate** – through the cold winter.

**So then they come out again in the spring?**

Some do. But in most firefly species, the larvae stay hidden for a *couple* of winters, emerging two or more years later and growing into fat grubs with glowing tails, which some people call **glow-worms**. As spring turns into summer, the grubs stop eating, build a protective cocoon (or **pupa**) around themselves, and spend a week or so rebuilding their bodies into a new shape. When they finally bust out of the pupa, they have transformed into adult **fireflies** (or **lightning bugs**) with hard bodies, glowing bellies, and buzzing wings.

**I'm confused – what are fireflies, anyway? Are they flies, worms, bugs, or what?**

Actually, they're none of those! They are a type of **beetle**, of the insect order **Coleoptera**. Beetles are

.....................................................................................

\* In some species, the grubs burrow into tree bark to hibernate, instead of going underground.

the most common type of insect on the planet. There are over 400,000 known species of beetle worldwide. Like all insects, they have **six legs** and **three** separate **body sections** – **head**, **thorax**, and **abdomen**. But unlike most other flying insects, a beetle's front wings are hardened into shell-like wing-covers (called **elytra**). These tough cases slide over their hind wings and protect them from damage when they're not in use.

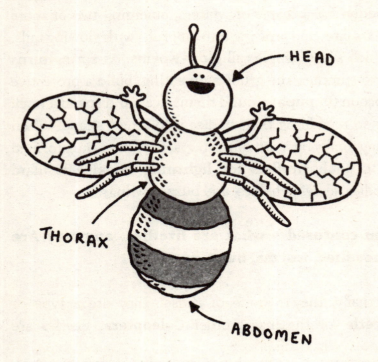

HEAD

THORAX

ABDOMEN

## So why do we call them flies, worms, and bugs?

Because, like most animals on the planet, fireflies take on **different shapes** for different stages in their **life cycle** (and some of those shapes happen to look a bit like worms, bugs, or flies).

While birds, mammals, and reptiles go straight from **egg** to **baby animal**, most other classes of animal – including **starfish, jellyfish, insects**, and **amphibians** – go through one or more **stages** in between.

You've probably seen **tadpoles** hatch from frog eggs at the pond. Well, tadpoles are the **larval** stage of frogs. They **look** and **act** different from adult frogs, and mostly swim about eating things and avoiding predators until they grow legs and mature into adults.

Many insects have an in-between stage called a **pupa (a cocoon)**, in which the larva dramatically reshapes itself into a very different shape, in a process called *metamorphosis* (which means 'change shape' in ancient Greek).

In the butterfly life cycle, the eggs hatch into wriggly **larvae** (caterpillars), which later **pupate** (make cocoons) and undergo **metamorphosis** to become adult butterflies. The adults lay eggs, and on the cycle goes.

In the **firefly** life cycle, the eggs hatch into predatory, slug-eating **larvae**, which burrow underground, emerge a few years later, **pupate**, and transform into adult fireflies. The interesting thing to note there is that because the newborn larvae stay underground for two or more years, the fireflies you see flashing and buzzing around this year are actually **two or more years old!** What's more, *their* babies won't take to the air as glowing, buzzing adults for another couple of years!

## Weirrrrrd. So why *do* fireflies flash their bottoms like that, anyway?

Simply put, they do it to attract other fireflies, in the hope they can find a mate and lay eggs before they die. (Remember – adult fireflies only live for a few short weeks. Only the *larvae* live on past the summer.) Each firefly species has its own flash-pattern, and some of them **synchronize** their flashes to create spectacular light shows that ripple and pulse across forests and mountainsides. By teaming up like this, the males invite a *bunch* of females to the party, increasing their chances of finding a mate.

**But how do they do it? Do they have bio-batteries or something?**

Not quite. They make two bioluminescent chemicals called **luciferin** and **luciferase**, and store them in special **light organs** in their bellies. There, the two proteins are combined with **oxygen** and chemical energy to create bursts of light. By controlling the flow of oxygen and chemicals to its light organs, the firefly can control the pattern of its flashes – even mimicking the patterns of other species.

**Cool. What if humans could do that? We could go camping without flashlights, read under the covers, find each other in the dark!**

Hmmm – I suppose so. But there's one fatal flaw to your brilliant plan . . .

**What's that?**

You would have to walk backwards, and put your book beneath your bottom.

# FIREFLY FACTS

- There are over 2,000 species of firefly in the world.

- Fireflies can be found all over Europe, Asia, Africa, Australia, and the Americas – every continent except Antarctica!

- *Lamprigera* fireflies, which live in Southeast Asia, can grow to the size of your palm.

- Some fireflies don't flash at all. These 'dark' fireflies communicate with smells instead.

- Some female fireflies flash to attract males, only to *eat* them on arrival. This helps them build stronger eggs for their chosen mate (who they do not eat).

- Fireflies taste really bad to frogs and toads, but many frogs eat them anyway. Particularly greedy frogs, who can eat so many that they start to glow in the dark, can become a target for foxes and raccoons!

# WHY DO SOME ANIMALS EAT PLANTS, AND SOME EAT EACH OTHER?

All animals eat for the same reason – to get energy. Whether they are plant-eating grazers or meat-eating hunters, all animals need a daily supply of energy to move and maintain their bodies. They just go about getting that energy in different ways.

**Where does the energy come from in the first place?**

Almost always from the sun. Plants* absorb heat and light from the sun, combined with water and carbon dioxide from the air and soil, and turn it into sugars, fats, and proteins. In other words,

* Along with **plankton**, single-celled creatures called **protists**, and some types of **bacteria**. More about those in a minute . . .

plants transform the sun's energy into energy-rich **food**.

Food for **themselves**, and food for everything that **eats them**.

So when a **sheep** or a **horse** eats grass, it is absorbing the energy from sunlight – pre-packaged by the grass into a tasty chemical form. It then uses that energy to move, breathe, build its own body, and (eventually) make more sheep and horses.

**So plants contain energy . . .**

Right.

**. . . and animals can get energy by eating the plants?**

Correct.

**So then why don't they *all* just eat plants? Why do lions eat antelopes? Why do anteaters eat ants? And why do humans eat animals *and* plants?**

That's a good question. One answer is that **not every animal *can* eat plants**. Lions, like all cats, are meat-eaters (or **carnivores**). Not only do they *like* to eat meat, they *have* to. Because their guts are **not made** for digesting plants, and they will get sick and die if they try to survive on leaves or grass.

Another answer to that question is that eating other animals is, sadly, **more efficient** than grazing on plants all day long. Plant-eaters like sheep, horses, and antelopes have to spend **all day** grazing on grass in order to get enough energy to power their bodies. It's a non-stop feeding effort that doesn't leave much time for anything else. But when a carnivore (**predator**) eats a herbivore (**prey** animal), it gets all that hard-earned energy all at once. Afterwards, the predator can afford to lounge around, skip a meal or two, rest and recover instead of chasing things all day long. In a way, carnivores are **cheats** – stealing the energy that plants and herbivores worked so hard to gather.

Of course, the chain may not stop there. Some predatory animals are also **food for other predators**, who hunt **them** in the hope of stealing *their* energy.

## Like big fish eating little fish?

Exactly. In the ocean, the picture might look something like this:

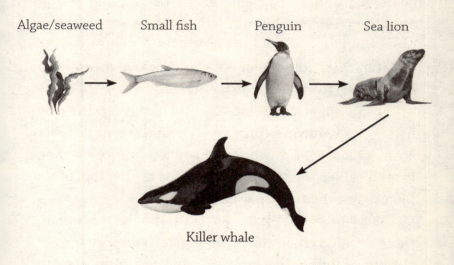

Algae/seaweed    Small fish    Penguin    Sea lion

Killer whale

- **Seaweed** turns sunlight into food (its own leaves) >
- **Fish** nibbles on the seaweed >
- **Penguin** eats the fish >
- **Sea lion** eats the penguin >
- **Killer whale** eats the sea lion

Biologists call this a **food chain**. All food chains start at the bottom with a **producer** (something that

**produces food** from sunlight). From there, the energy flows through one or more **consumers** (things that eat other things for energy), until it ends with an **animal that nothing else eats** (or has **no predators** of its own). In every chain, plants or bacteria are the producers, and **herbivores** are the first (or primary) consumers.

After that, you get one or more **carnivores** (also consumers) feeding on the herbivores.

In this chain, the seaweed is the producer, the tiny fish is the herbivore (primary consumer) and the rest are all predatory carnivores (consumers). Since nothing eats the killer whale, we say that it is at the 'top' of its food chain. The **top**, or **apex predator**.

Everywhere on Earth, on land and in the ocean, there are food chains like this, in which **energy moves through living systems** – from **producers** to **consumers**, from **plants** to **herbivores**, from **herbivores** to **carnivores**, and from **carnivores** to **apex predators**.

## So are most animals herbivores or carnivores?

Because of the way energy flows through the chain, there are way more plants than herbivores, way more herbivores than carnivores, and very few apex predators. This is why there are way more **ants** than **anteaters**, and more **antelopes** than **lions**.

Food chains **help us to understand living systems**. For example, if there is no rain for many months and the plants (producers) at the bottom of the chain fail to grow, then the herbivores start to die off. If the number of herbivores drops, then the predators will have trouble catching enough food, and *they* will start to disappear, too.

So by watching the top predators in a food chain, we can get an idea of **how healthy the whole system is**. If the apex predators start to disappear, then we know something is **wrong** further down the chain. If there are **fewer killer whales** and **polar bears** around, that probably means there are **fewer seals**. If there are fewer seals, then there are **fewer fish**. If there are fewer fish, then maybe we should check whether we are **fishing too much** in that area, or if something is **polluting** the ocean and **stopping sea plants from growing**.

**How do food chains end, then? Do they just stop at the top predator?**

In one way, yes. But in another way, they *never* end, because eventually – even if nothing hunts and kills it – the predator at the top of the food chain will die of disease or old age. When that happens, its energy-rich body will be eaten by **scavengers** (like crabs, vultures, and hyenas), or broken down by **decomposers** (bacteria and fungi). Every living thing in every chain – from the plants at the bottom to the herbivores and carnivores further up the chain – will be scavenged or decomposed in this way. This **recycles** the energy trapped at the top of the food chain – putting it back into the ground or ocean, where **microscopic bacteria and fungi** feed a new chain of plants, herbivores, and predators.

Also, no food chain exists **all on its own**. Most **consumers** eat more than one type of **plant**, many **predators** eat more than one kind of **prey** animal, and some animals – like us – **eat both plants and animals** for energy. In this way, food chains weave and loop together into complex **food webs**, with **hundreds** or **thousands** of different living species all depending on each other for survival.

**Wow. I never thought about it like that.**

Yep. The world is a big, beautiful, complicated place, and we humans are just **one small part** of it. Once in a while, we get a bit too big for our boots, and nature reminds us of that. But if we take some time to understand our planet, and all the living things that live alongside us, maybe we can hang around for a few million years more. Together.

# NORTH AMERICAN FOOD CHAIN

How many more animals might be part of this food chain?

_____
_____
_____
_____
_____

Which animals are the apex predators in this picture?

_____
_____
_____
_____
_____

What might a food chain look like where you are?

_____
_____
_____
_____
_____

FUN

## Tertiary Consumers

Coyote

Mountain lion

Bobcat

## Secondary Consumers

Ringtail

Western whiptail

Raven

Black tipped jackrabbit

Pine marten

## Primary Consumers

Pika

Red -breasted nuthatch

Pacific tree frog

Edith checkerspot

Douglas's squirrel

Mule deer

## Producers and Decomposers

Plants, Flowers, nuts, seeds, fruit, insects

# WHY DO SOME VOLCANOES ERUPT (BUT OTHERS DON'T)?

Volcanoes are dangerous and mysterious things. They can sleep quietly for hundreds or thousands of years before exploding into action. It all depends on how the volcano is formed and what is happening far beneath the surface. And although we can never know for certain, we can guess which ones are dead, and which ones are still very much alive.

**Wait – volcanoes are *alive*?**

No, not really. Volcanoes do not actually live, sleep, or die. They are huge piles of lava and ash – not living things. But in many ways they *act* like living things – showing activity and movement for short bursts of time, then lying silent and still in between.

Cinder Cone Volcanoes

Composite Volcanoes

Shield Volcanoes

Lava Domes

Volcanoes, though, have much longer lifespans than we do. It can take anywhere from **10,000** to **500,000 years** for a volcano to form, and they can stay active for **millions of years** before finally sputtering out.

## How are volcanoes formed?

All volcanoes are formed by hot, liquid rock (or **magma**) and gases bubbling up from the Earth's interior (or **mantle**), and escaping through a hole in its solid **crust**.

This usually happens where pieces of the Earth's crust – called **tectonic plates** – move apart from each other, allowing magma to rise up and fill the spaces in between. But it can also happen where plates move **towards** each other, and one slips beneath the other, pushing magma upward through the crust in the process. Plate boundaries like this run through the middle of **Japan**, **Indonesia** and **New Zealand**, which is why these countries have so many volcanoes (some Japanese and Indonesian islands literally are volcanoes!).

But volcanoes can also form over tiny **hotspots** in the **middle** of a crusty plate – creating a **chain** of volcanoes as the plate moves along, like blobs of icing on a cake. The volcanic islands of **Hawaii** were formed this way, and new islands are *still* oozing from the hotspot there!

## Okay, but why are they shaped like giant cones?

Once it clears the surface, the magma rising up through the crust either **oozes** out as semi-liquid **lava**<sup>*</sup>, or **bursts** out in an explosion of gas, rock, and

...............................................................................

\* Molten rock *beneath* the ground (or *inside* the Earth) is called magma, but once it's above ground (or *out* of the Earth) we call it lava. Same stuff, two names.

ash. Over thousands of years, **layers** of rock, ash, and lava pile around the hole to form a **cone**.

Some (called **shield volcanoes**) form **wide, flat** cones. Others (called **cinder cones**) have **short, steep** cones less than 300 m tall. The largest volcanoes (called **composite volcanoes**, or **stratovolcanoes**) are huge, cone-shaped mountains thousands of metres tall. Japan's famous **Mount Fuji** (**3,777 m** or **12,388 feet tall**) is one of these. The shape of a volcano depends on how thick and gloopy its magma (or lava) is.

**So why do some of them just ooze lava, but others blow up?**

How a volcano **erupts** depends partly on the gloopiness (or **viscosity**) of its **magma**, and how much **gas** it contains.

If the magma is **runny** and has only a **little** gas in it, then it escapes the hole (or vent) in the volcano fairly easily, without too much pressure building up. This kind of volcano will **erupt gently** for many years, dribbling lava down its sides at a steady rate. Many of the volcanoes in Hawaii are like this.

But if the magma is **gloopy** (or **viscous**), and had a **lot** of gas trapped in it, then when it reaches the vent it can get stuck and temporarily plug the hole. Over many years (anywhere from 10 to 100,000 years or more), the pressure beneath the plug builds up. Eventually, it **explodes**, sending a huge cloud of super-heated gas way up into the atmosphere and showering hot rock and ash for **miles** around. Italy's famous Mount Vesuvius **erupted violently** like this in AD 79, destroying the nearby Roman city of Pompeii.

**Whoa! So how do we know which ones are safe, and which ones are ticking time-bombs?!**

Well, we can't know for sure. But we can take a solid guess, based on how they are behaving right now, and how they have been behaving lately.

Scientists who study volcanoes – called **vulcanologists** – have three categories for volcanoes.

**Active** volcanoes are those that are spewing lava and volcanic gases, or only recently stopped doing so. If it is leaking, oozing, dribbling or exploding *right now*, it is obviously an active volcano. But active volcanoes can also lay **dormant** for a while. Which brings us to the second category . . .

**Dormant** volcanoes are not currently erupting, but still show signs that they *might*. These signs include

**mini-earthquakes** in the area of the volcano, or subtle changes in the **gases** venting out of their craters or sides. Generally speaking, if a volcano has erupted within the last 10,000 years – which is a pretty long time – then it is thought to be dormant, or *potentially* active. If it has been longer than that, then it is considered **extinct**.

**Extinct** volcanoes have never erupted within recorded human history – not in **medieval** times, not in **Roman** times, or even ancient **Egyptian** times. Most have not erupted for 10,000 years or more – since the end of the last ice age. When a volcano is extinct, it shows no signs of activity – no tremors, no gases, nothing at all.

Active Volcanoes   Dormant Volcanoes   Extinct Volcanoes

**So how many volcanoes are there, and how many of them are still active?**

In all, there are over **1,500** active or dormant volcanoes in the world today. Of those, around **600** have erupted within the last 2,000 years. The rest, within the last 10,000 years. About 50-70 volcanoes become or remain active each year, and at any given time an average of **20** volcanoes are erupting. In other words: ***right now, as you are reading these words***, there are probably at least **20** volcanoes popping their fiery tops across the planet.

**Active** volcanoes include Mount **Etna** (Italy), **Santorini** (Greece), Mount **Erebus** (Antarctica), **Mauna Loa** (Hawaii), **Fuego** (Guatemala), **Kick 'Em Jenny** (Grenada), and **Michael** (Sandwich Islands).

**Dormant** volcanoes include Mount **Hood** (USA), Mount **Kilimanjaro** (Tanzania), Mount **Edziza** (Canada) and **Mauna Kea** (Hawaii).

**Extinct** volcanoes include **Ben Nevis** (the tallest mountain in Scotland), **Arthur's Seat** (which overlooks the city of Edinburgh), **Black Butte** (USA), **Fuerteventura** (Canary Islands), **Kauai** (Hawaii), **Mount Terror** (Antarctica), and the aptly named **Boring Lava Field** (USA).

But here's the thing: sometimes we get it wrong. Volcanoes can *appear* dormant – or even extinct –

while remaining very active below the surface. Mount **Vesuvius** was thought to be extinct when it destroyed Pompeii in AD 79. Mount **Pinatabo** was thought to be dormant when it erupted in the Philippines in 1991. As was Mount **St Helens** (USA, 1980), and the **Soufriere Hills** (Monserrat, 1995).

The point is – **you can never trust a volcano**.

**I guess not!**

# VOLCANOES: CONES OF DOOM

- As if it wasn't scary enough, an erupting volcano can also trigger deadly **earthquakes**, **tsunamis**, **flash floods**, and **mudflows**.

- **More than three quarters of all volcanic eruptions happen underwater.** Many are at mid-ocean ridges where tectonic plates spread apart to create new seafloor.

- More than **half** of the world's **active** volcanoes lie within the **Ring of Fire** – a region that encircles the Pacific Ocean from Japan to Australia to the western Americas.

- The deadliest eruption in recent history happened in Indonesia in **1883**, when the volcanic island of **Krakatoa** erupted – creating a tsunami that killed 36,000 people. The explosion was so loud it was heard in Australia and Mauritius – both thousands of miles away.

- Though most volcanoes take thousands of years to form, some can literally spring up overnight. On 20 February 1943, a cinder cone volcano named **Paricutin** appeared in a cornfield in Mexico. Within a week, it was the size of a five-storey building, and by the end of the year, it was **336 m** (**1,100 feet**) tall.

# HOW DO CLOUDS MAKE LIGHTNING?

Lightning is a powerful electric current that forms naturally in thunderclouds, and flows between clouds and the ground. It is created by the massive build-up of electric charge inside a cloud, which eventually discharges itself in the form of a lightning bolt.

Most of the time, those bolts stay within the cloud itself. But sometimes, they find their way to the ground – ripping the air apart as they go.

**That's crazy. What's actually *in* a thundercloud that makes it all electrified?**

Nothing special. Just millions of tiny droplets of water and ice, suspended in the air. Which is basically what *all* clouds are.

Clouds are formed as heat from the sun **evaporates**

water from rivers, lakes, and oceans. When this happens, the **liquid** water turns into a **gas** (called **water vapour**), which rises up – far away from the ground – until it reaches colder air higher up in the sky. From there, clouds are blown around by shifting air currents (or as we usually call them, **winds**), splitting, combining, growing, changing shape, and moving over land and sea at various heights (or **altitudes**).

Depending on where the cloud ends up, different things can happen to it. Many clouds cool off and dump their water back to the ground as **rain**, **sleet**, or **snow**. This returns water to the ground, forming new rivers and lakes on its way to the ocean – completing the water cycle all living things depend on. Alternatively, the cloud might spread out into a low-lying **mist** or **fog**, which clings to the ground in big, soggy droplets. Or if a cloud grows big and tall enough, it might turn into a monster **thundercloud,** pelting us with rain, hail, and lightning.

## So can any kind of cloud make lightning?

Nope – only the ones that grow big and dense enough to do so. These start off as small, fluffy **cumulus** clouds which swell and expand, reaching high into the atmosphere to become dark, towering **cumulonimbus** clouds. The upper reaches of these clouds freeze first,

133

turning the water droplets suspended there into tiny particles of **ice**. As the cloud grows, these ice particles bump and smash into each other more often, creating a **build-up of electric charges** – some **positive**, some **negative**. The positive ones rise to the top of the cloud, while the negative ones move to the bottom. If the cloud is very large, then the build-up of charges at the top and bottom of the cloud becomes **massive**. Eventually, a giant **spark** forms between the two parts of the cloud, and arcs between them in a temporary electric current. The power of this current is so huge that it literally **rips the air molecules apart** as it goes, creating a bright flash of light (**lightning**) and massive soundwaves in the air for miles around (**thunder**). Because light travels much faster than sound, we see the **flash of lightning first**, and hear the **boom of thunder later**.

Most of the time, these lightning bolts **stay within the cloud itself**, making thunderclouds flash and flicker in the sky. It can also arc from one cloud to another, forming **cloud-to-cloud lightning**. Lightning that stays in the sky like this is sometimes called **sheet lightning** or **heat lightning**. But every so often, a current forms between the cloud and the ground, creating the beautiful (but scary) **fork lightning** we all hide from.

**Why does it zigzag through the sky, instead of just going in a straight line to the ground?**

Because the current is trying to find the easiest path through the air, from the built-up negative charges in the underside of the cloud to the built-up positive charges in the ground below. Air is not a perfect mixture of gases. It contains tonnes of dust particles, pollutants, all kinds of stuff, and it does not actually **conduct** electricity that well. So the electric current splits, arcs, and zigzags around pockets of **resistance** in the air until it finds an easy way through.

Also the electric current that forms between the cloud and ground **flows both ways**. As negative charges from the cloud flow downward, positive charges on the ground reach upward, seeking their **own path of least resistance** through **anything sticking up from the ground**. This could be a **tree**, a **radio antenna**, or a **building**. This is why many tall buildings have **lightning conductors** to draw the current safely through their structures.

It is also why you should move indoors if you hear thunder or see lightning. Because out in it, if *you* are the tallest thing around, then the lightning could move through *you* instead.

**But as long as there are no thunderclouds in the sky, you're okay, right? I mean, can lightning happen *without* clouds?**

Well, no. Lightning cannot form in a clear, blue sky, all by itself. Without the charged ice particles contained in clouds, there can be no electric current, and no lightning. But lightning can still sometimes strike from a sky that *looks* clear. This is because – as we already saw – lightning rarely travels straight down to the ground. On

its search for a clear channel through the air, it can arc and zigzag over **40 km (25 miles)** from the cloud that produced it. In other words, the storm might be too far off to see, and the lightning can race ahead of it. This is why you should head indoors **when you hear the distant rumbles of thunder** – not wait until the dark clouds move overhead. Long distance lightning strikes like this – called '**bolts from the blue**' – are rare, but they do happen.

**Yikes. What would happen if you got hit by lightning? Would it burn you to a crisp?**

Not necessarily. Many people have actually survived being struck by lightning (a few of them, more than once!). It depends **how** and **where** you get hit.

In a **direct strike**, the lightning goes straight through your body – with some of the massive charge moving across your skin, and the rest going through your blood vessels and nervous system. This can be enough to **stop your heart** or **damage your brain** beyond repair. At the very least, you would get **massive burns** where the lightning went in and out of your body. It can also heat up **metal belt buckles** and **jewellery**, creating burns around those. You may also end up with serious **hearing loss**, as the boom of exploding air pressure around the lightning bolt smashes through your delicate **eardrums**.

**Yowch!**

Indeed. But there are other ways to get hit, besides directly.

In a **splash strike**, lightning arcs from a nearby object (like a tree or electric pylon) and only part of the current goes through you. These can be deadly too –

which is why hiding under trees in a thunderstorm is not the best idea either.

In a **ground strike**, lightning hits the ground nearby, and part of the current travels through the ground and up into your body from there. And in a **conduction** strike, lightning moves sideways through a metal object – like electrical wiring in a building, or a metal fence outdoor – to hit you far from the strike point.

People survive **splash, ground,** and **conduction strikes** more often than they do **direct** ones. But frankly, **none** of them are fun.

Thankfully, direct lightning strikes on people are rare. Most buildings, cars, and aeroplanes will channel lightning safely around you if they are struck, so unless you are caught out in the open during a thunderstorm – chances are you will live your entire life zap-free.

# LIGHTNING FACTS

- The average **width of a lightning bolt** is about **2–3 cm**, which is roughly the width of your thumb. The average **length** of a lightning bolt is **3–5 km** (**2–3 miles**).

- Lightning travels through the air at around **270,000 mph**, and temporarily heats the air to between **8,000** and **33,000°C** (**15,000** and **60,000 °F**). Hotter than the surface of the sun.

- Zoom out and watch the whole planet at once, and you'll see lightning crackling all over the place. It strikes the Earth around **3 million times per day** – that's roughly **44 times every second**.

- When lightning hits a **tree**, it can **superheat** the liquid sap running through it, causing it to explode – splitting the wood and **blasting its bark right off**.

- Lightning can (and does) **strike twice in the same place**. In fact, each flash of lightning we see is often **20** or more strikes per second, to and from the *exact same place*.

- Your chances of getting hit in a **single year** are about **1 in 700,000**. Your chances of being struck at *any* time in your **entire life** is about **1 in 3,000**.

- Wearing **rubber shoes** or **boots** does **not** protect you from lightning strikes. At all.

# WHY IS CLIMATE CHANGE SO BAD?

Having the planet warm up a bit might not *seem* so bad – especially if you hate chilly weather. But if our atmosphere keeps warming and changing, it will cause massive rearrangements in all the living landscapes of our world. Depending on what we do about all this – *right now* – our future lives on Earth could be very bright, or very bleak.

**Yikes. That doesn't sound good. So what *is* climate change, really?**

What have you heard about it?

**Well, I know it has something to do with the poles heating up. Like, the Arctic and Antarctic are melting, so the animals there have less ice to live on.**

That is part of it, yes. But it's not just the ice caps that are heating up. The whole *planet* is. Or rather, our **atmosphere** is warming and changing, which is altering local climates and weather patterns everywhere on Earth. As far as we can tell, this has been happening for at *least* 100 years. And for the last **50 years** in particular, temperatures have been *racing* up worldwide.

**But why is that happening? Is the sun getting hotter or something?**

That could be one explanation. But scientists have looked into it, and the amount of light and heat (or radiation) coming from the sun has not changed much at all in the last 60–100 years. If anything, the sun is kicking out *less* radiation lately.

**So if it's not the sun, then what is it?**

Apparently, something happened to our gassy atmosphere in the last 100-odd years, making it **thicker** and **warmer** – like a **blanket that traps too much heat** and will not allow the lands and oceans beneath to cool off. Any idea what might have caused that change?

Here's a clue: Before 1900, most of us still got around on two feet – or maybe four feet – rather than four wheels . . .

## Cars! We invented cars!

Bingo. Or rather, we invented petrol and gas-powered engines, and started shoving them into **cars**, **trains**, and **aeroplanes**. This connected us across countries and continents, and changed the face of travel forever. Unfortunately, it also changed the Earth's atmosphere, too – adding **billions** of tonnes of exhaust gases into the air every year.

Of course, it probably did not *start* with cars. We had already been using **coal-powered engines** in **factories**, **steam trains** and **steam ships** for a century before fancy petrol engines[*] and jet engines came along. Burning all that coal almost certainly contributed to the altered atmosphere we have now (and still does, where coal and gas are burned in power plants to create electricity). But adding *billions* of cars and aeroplanes to our roads and skies

......................................................................................

[*] Technically, these are called internal combustion engines, as they create movement by burning fuel *inside* the engine, in lots of tiny, popping explosions. As opposed to steam engines, which burn coal *outside* the engine, and pump steam into pistons to create movement. So there you go.

is likely the cause of the faster changes we have seen since 1900.

This is because the vast majority of our cars, aeroplanes, and power plants all burn **fossil fuels**. These are fuels made from the bodies of ancient, living creatures – smashed and liquified over millions of years beneath the weight of the land or ocean. When we pull these out of the ground, **concentrate** them, and **burn** them in engines and power plants, we release millions of years worth, and millions of bodies worth, of trapped energy. And along with it, vast amounts of the waste gases **carbon dioxide** and **methane**.

It is *these* gases, scientists say, that have been changing the Earth's atmosphere, and are steadily making our planet too cozy for comfort. And this is already creating big problems.

## What kind of problems?

We are already seeing big changes in **global temperatures** and **weather patterns**. Hot places are getting hotter, wet places even wetter, and dry places even drier. In countries across the globe, every year sees new records for 'hottest day' or 'hottest month' ever measured. In the rainy places, **flooding** and **tropical storms** are getting worse. In the dry places,

**droughts** and **wildfires** are becoming larger and more common.

Nearer the poles, **ice sheets and glaciers are melting**, leaving polar animals without habitat and hunting grounds, and dumping billions of tonnes of water into the oceans. This is gradually raising sea levels around the world. If this continues, sea levels could be **30 cm (12 inches)** higher by 2030, and **70 cm (2.3 feet)** higher by 2100.

**Just a couple of feet? That doesn't seem so bad.**

That depends where you live. Sea level rise is already causing more flooding in low-lying places like Vietnam, the Netherlands, and Venice. By 2100, low-lying islands like **Tuvalu** and the **Maldives** will be partly submerged and impossible to live on. And if the sea-level keeps rising into the next century, coastal cities like **New York**, **Shanghai**, and **Rio de Janeiro** will be flooded – as will cities on tidal rivers like **Cairo** and **London**.

Eventually, as low-lying places get flooded, people and animals will have to move to higher ground, pack closer together, compete over land, fresh water, and other resources. Animal species worldwide will go extinct, and packed-in human populations will see more droughts, diseases, and conflicts.

**Yeesh. Not good. So what can we do about all this?**

Firstly, we have to stop making it worse. We have to cut down on carbon dioxide emissions, by changing the way we power our cars, planes, and trains. If we build and use more **electric** and **hydrogen-powered** vehicles, then this will be a good start.

That said, that electricity and hydrogen fuel **has to come from somewhere**. If we keep burning **coal**, **gas**, and **oil** to create electricity, then switching to electric cars and trains is pretty much pointless. For this reason, we need to change our **entire way of producing and using energy**. We have to shift to using **renewable**

**energy** sources like **solar**, **wind**, and **wave power**. Only *then* can we stop burning fossil fuels, and the massive carbon-dioxide-dump that creates.

Besides changing our energy sources, there are many other important things we have to do, too. Like **slow the burning and logging of our forests**. Trees and plants suck carbon dioxide from the atmosphere and dump it back into their bodies and the ground. So forests are like massive air filters – cleaning the air and protecting us from the effects of climate change. If we burn them or chop them all down, the filters will be gone, and the air will get thicker and thicker with carbon dioxide.

The good news is, we can **plant new trees and forests** to replace the old ones. We can **protect the animals** that are losing habitats to climate change. We can **build and drive more electric cars and trains**. And we can change our towns and cities to become **cleaner, greener places**. And in many countries, this is already happening.

**Sweden** aims to be the first country to get rid of fossil fuels completely, with **100%** renewable-energy towns and vehicles by 2040.

**Costa Rica** already gets **95%** of its energy from solar, geothermal, and hydroelectric sources, and is on track to go **totally fossil-free** by 2022.

**Scotland** just built the world's largest floating wind

farm, generating **98%** of its electricity in the windier months.

And more than **half** the electricity in **Denmark**, **Germany**, **Morocco**, and **Kenya** comes from renewable sources.

Countries are coming together to fight climate change, remaking our world to be a better place for everyone. We just need to keep going, and make sure everyone joins in.

After all – for now at least – we only have one planet to live on. So we'd better look after it.

# TRY IT YOURSELF: CREATE YOUR OWN WATER CYCLE

To illustrate the water cycle, try this easy at-home experiment.

**You will need:**

- a ziplock plastic sandwich-sized bag
- a black permanent marker
- clear tape
- a cup of water with a drop of blue food dye in it

First, draw the sun and clouds at the top of the bag with permanent marker.

Pour the cup of blue water into the bag and seal it closed.

Tape the bag to a window which gets direct sun and observe the bag for at least a day.

As the water heats up, you will see the evaporation of the water into the clouds, then dripping back down to the water below as 'rain' or precipitation.

ziplock plastic bag

blue water

# QUICK ONES –
# FORESTS, TREES, AND MAN-EATING PLANTS

**Where are the world's biggest forests?**

The largest forests in the world are the **Amazon**, the **Taiga**, and the **Congo Basin**.

The **Amazon rainforest** is in South America. It is over 55 million years old and contains over **390 million trees**, spread across **5.5 million square kilometres (2 million square miles)**. The forest is so huge that it spans **eight** countries – Brazil, Bolivia, Peru, Ecuador, Colombia, Venezuela, Guyana, and Suriname, plus

French Guiana, which is an overseas territory. **10% of all the known animal species on Earth** live there – including jaguars, spider monkeys, toucans, sloths, and tarantulas. This makes it a critically important **habitat for vulnerable species**, as well as being a **massive carbon dioxide filter** that protects us from climate change. Which is why we need to protect it at all costs.

After the Amazon, the next **three** largest forests are all in the **Taiga** (or **Boreal Forest**) – which stretches **7,000 km (4,300 miles)** from **Norway** to **Siberia**, and right across **Canada**. The Taiga was once a single forest, but it split in two when the continents drifted apart millions of years ago. The Taiga makes up around **one third of all the world's forest resources**, and absorbs more carbon dioxide than **all the world's tropical rainforests put together**. Temperatures there drop below **-40°C (-40°F)** in winter, and it is home to thousands of animal species, including bears, wolves, foxes, beavers, and pine martens.

## What's the biggest tree in the world?

The world's biggest tree is a **quaking aspen** called **Pando**, found in Fishlake National Forest, Colorado, USA. Pando looks more like a small **forest** or **wood**, covering half a square kilometre (0.2 square miles). But tests have revealed that every tree in that wood is an identical clone with a single, connected root system, making Pando a single, living organism or tree. If you buy that definition, then Pando is over 80,000 years old, weighs 6,600 tons, and is by far the largest tree in the world.

If not, and you are looking for the largest, free-standing trunk in the world, then that record goes to one of two **giant redwood** trees, both found in California, USA. The **tallest** tree is **Hyperion**, found in Redwood National Park. Hyperion is over **116 m (380 feet)** tall – taller than the famous Statue of Liberty. The **widest** is the General Sherman tree, found in Kings Canyon National Park. The General is an impressive **83 m (272 feet) tall**, and over **11 m (36 feet) wide**. That's roughly as wide as **four** London buses.

## Why don't plants grow in the desert?

Most plants need five things to grow: **light**, **air**, **water**, **nutrients (from soil)**, and **room to grow**. Although there is plenty of light, air and room in the desert, **water** and **soil** are scarce. Worse yet, temperatures in the desert can swing from a withering **40°C (106°F)** in the daytime to a frosty **-4°C (25°F)** by night. But incredibly, some plants still do grow in the desert. Especially **succulent** plants like **aloe**, **agave**, and **cactus**.

Succulents suck up as much water as they can and **store** it in their roots, leaves and stems. They also have a **waxy coating** that seals in moisture and prevents water loss by **evaporation**. To top it all off, many have **prickly skins and spines** to deter thirsty animals – including humans. So if you ever get stuck in the desert, crack open a cactus for a drink. Just don't get jabbed in the process.

## Can a plant grow without soil?

Yes, they can. But only as long as it can get water and nutrients from somewhere *other* than the soil. All plants need **water and nutrients** to grow, and most plants suck them from the soil using their hairy **roots**. From there, it moves through a network of tubes called **xylem,** up through their **stems** to their **leaves**. There, water leaks and evaporates out through tiny holes called **stomata**, which the plant can open and close throughout the day. Nutrients, meanwhile, are essential for plant growth. Without them, the plant cannot grow, survive, or convert air, water, and sunlight into plant sugars (which are then transported back down through the plants in tubes called **phloem**).

To grow a plant without soil, you have to use a special, ready-made solution of water, minerals and nutrients, which contains everything the plant needs. This is called **hydroponic** growth, and with a little experimentation, many types of plant can be made to grow this way. Scientists are currently researching how to use this method for growing food plants in space – which may be necessary if we are going to take longer journeys and colonize other planets!

**Are there any plants that eat people?**

No – none that we know of. But **there *are* some meat-eating plants** – or plants that trap and eat animals for nutrients. These include **pitcher plants**, which are shaped like tall jugs (or **pitchers**) filled with a sticky-sweet juice that attracts insects, frogs, and rats. When an animal steps on its slippery leaves, they fall in and are unable to climb out. Trapped inside, they are slowly drowned and digested by the plant's juices – a truly horrible way to go. Other carnivorous plants include **Venus flytraps,** which have tough, spring-loaded leaves that snap shut on flies and other insects, trapping and digesting them inside. But thankfully, none of these carnivorous plants is anywhere near large enough to trap a human.

The truly disgusting **corpse flower** was once *thought* to eat people, but definitely does not. Rather, it releases a **foul odour** that makes it smell like a cross between **old cheese, rotting fish, sweaty socks,** and **poo**. This attracts flies and dung beetles, which help to **pollinate** the flower as they carry its pollen from one foul-smelling plant to another.

So the only **man-eating plants** that exist on Earth are in science-fiction stories.

But who knows? Maybe on some other planet – far, far away – huge, alien plants are waiting to meet us . . . and eat us!

# SNAP, CRACKLE, AND BOOM

WHEEEE!

# WHY DOES YOUR SHADOW CHANGE SHAPE?

Shadows are made when beams of light are blocked by a solid object before they can reach the wall, ground, or other surface beyond it. During the daytime, your own shadow is created when your body blocks sunlight. But the sun shifts higher and lower in the sky during the day, changing the length of the shadows it creates.

**Hold on – if the sun makes shadows, then why do we still see shadows at night?**

Because the sun might be our *main* source of light, it is not the *only* light source in the world. After sunset, some beams of sunlight are bounced off the moon, creating beams of reflected **moonlight**. Burning fires and candles release both heat and light, creating flickering shadows by **firelight** and **candlelight**. And for at least 150 years, we have been using electricity to create **electric lights** – including electric **streetlights**, **headlights** on cars, and battery-powered **torches** or **flashlights**. Any of these light sources can make shadows, in the right conditions.

Making shadows is simple. Light travels in straight lines from a light source to an object.

Some beams of light **miss the object**, passing close by its edges, and hit the surface behind it. Other light beams **hit the object**, and do not make it to the surface behind. **Where the light is blocked, you get dark, unlit patches** on the surface, with the **exact same outline** as the object blocking the light. Et voilà – a perfect shadow.

**But shadows aren't perfect, are they?**

How do you mean?

**Well, they might be *sort* of the same shape as you. But they also stretch and shrink. Sometimes, your shadow looks taller than you, and sometimes it looks short and fat. Why is that?**

That is because the position of the sun (the source of light that creates your shadow) changes throughout the course of the day. This changes the angle of the light beams as they hit your body, squashing or stretching the outline of your shadow.

Close to **dawn**, the sun appears **low in the sky.** The light from it hits you almost sideways, casting **long shadows** behind you (and behind everything else). By **noon**, the sun is much **higher in the sky**, and light from it is coming **straight down** on your head (or at least, more vertically than horizontally). This makes your shadow more **short** and **squat**.

SMALL ANGLE

LARGE ANGLE

SHORT SHADOW

LONG SHADOW

As the sun continues its arc across the sky and dips down towards the horizon near **sunset**, the light is travelling **sideways** again, making your shadow **longer** once more.

If you look closely, you will also notice that the length of your **shadow changes from season to season**, as the sun's path is much **lower** in the sky in **winter**, and much **higher** in **summer**. It also depends on **how far north or south of the equator you live**, because that changes the angles between the sun and your spot on the Earth.

**But if objects block light to make shadows, then why are shadows greyish, and not, like, *totally* black?**

Because while *that* object is **blocking** light from the sun, *other* nearby objects could be **reflecting** it. This brightens or 'fills in' the shadow a little, making it less dark. Notice, though, that shadows made by moonlight and torchlight *are* pretty black. Because without the sun in the sky, there is lot less light bouncing around to fill in the shadows.

**Okay – so this might seem like a silly question . . . but does *everything* have a shadow? I mean – does anything *not* make shadows?**

Actually, that's not a silly question at all! Some objects *don't* have obvious shadows, because light can **flow straight through them**. It all depends on what the object is **made of**.

When it comes to light and shadows, you can put most materials into one of three groups: **transparent**, **translucent**, and **opaque**.

**Transparent materials** allow light to go straight through them. Pure water and air are transparent. So are clear glass and clear plastic sandwich bags.

**Translucent materials** let some light beams pass through, but block the rest. Stained glass windows, plastic milk containers, and the lenses of sunglasses are translucent. So are semi-clear liquids like cooking oil and white wine.

**Opaque materials** block most or all light that hits them. Wood, stone, cement, and most clothing fabrics are opaque[*].

Of course, transparent materials can be *made* opaque by adding things that block light. Water can be made translucent by adding a little opaque dye, or made completely opaque by adding mud. As you add these drop by drop, more and more light gets blocked, changing the material from transparent to opaque.

...................................................................................

[*] A good thing, too. Otherwise everyone could see right though your jeans and T-shirt!

**Can you do it the other way? Can you make things go *transparent*?**

Yes and no. Some types of materials can shift from opaque to transparent when you run an electric current through them. These are called **electrochromic** materials, and they are already being used to make **smart glass** (also known as **switch glass**) for car windscreens and aircraft windows.

Smart glass has millions of tiny liquid crystals inside it, which can either **block** or **transmit** light depending on **which way they are facing**. When you run a current through it, the crystals **rotate**, making it **opaque** (solid white or black), **translucent** (tinted), or **transparent**. Materials like this can also be layered, or made in different colours, so that the glass can take on many different appearances.

Technically, this is taking a **transparent** material and making it more or less **opaque**, rather than the other way around.

So far, we have not found any way of taking **opaque** things and changing their chemical structure to make them **transparent** or **invisible**. But who knows – maybe one day we will.

## SHADOWS AND LIGHT

● **Red**, **green**, and **blue** are the **primary colours** of light. Mixing them in different ways will make all the other colours – including white. Colour TVs and computer screens take advantage of this by using RGB (red, green, and blue) **pixels** – tiny coloured dots which light up in different ways to make whole images on the screen.

● There are actually **millions** of colours in a rainbow – we just name the **seven main groups** of colours that our human eyes can see (red, orange, yellow, green, blue, indigo, and violet).

● Many animals can see colours that are invisible to humans. Many birds, spiders, and insects can see **ultraviolet light** (sometimes called 'bee purple'), while many snakes can see **infrared light** (also known as heat radiation), allowing them to see the warm bodies of their prey in the cold, dark night.

● The brightest object in the known universe was discovered in 2019. It is a kind of star called a **quasar**, which sits in the centre of a galaxy roughly 12.8 billion light years away. Its light is **600 trillion** times brighter than the sun.

● The darkest material on Earth is called Vantablack. It was created by a team of British scientists in 2014, and it absorbs 99.96% of all visible, ultraviolet, and infrared light. It is made of tiny carbon nanotubes, which can be spray-painted onto any object to make it look like a black hole right out of a comic book!

WHEEEE!

# WHY DON'T MAGNETS STICK TO EVERYTHING?

Magnets are objects that can pull (attract) certain types of metal towards themselves, and attract or repel *other* magnets. Everything is a *little* bit magnetic. But very few materials have strong enough **magnetic fields** to act like magnets. And many materials – like wood, stone, and plastic – have fields too weak to be affected by them.

**Wait – what? What's a magnetic field?**

A **magnetic field** is the area around a magnet in which there is an obvious magnetic force.

It is caused by the **movement of charged particles** inside a material, which creates both electric and magnetic fields. Electricity and magnetism are actually part of the same force – called the **electromagnetic force** – which is one of the **four fundamental forces** in the universe*. This force explains everything from how atoms clump together to make **molecules** and **matter**, to how **light**, **heat**, and **electricity** move between objects.

In short, it's kind of a big deal.

All you need to know for now is that **magnetic fields surround magnetic objects**, and that they influence (push, pull, or direct) **electric charges**, **electric currents** and the **magnetic fields of other objects**. And they can do this at a **distance**.

How *far* the field reaches depends on how large and powerful the magnet is. Small, weak iron magnets might only pull on things a **few millimetres** away, while the **Earth's magnetic field** extends **600,000 km (370,000 miles)** out into space, and attracts and deflects charged particles from the sun and space all day long!

## Is that how magnets can pull on each other without touching?

Right. The magnetic field of one object pulls or pushes on the field of another. And since both fields extend

---

* The others being **gravity**, and the **strong** and **weak nuclear forces** that hold the core of every atom together.

some distance away from the surfaces of the objects, they do not need to be touching for the pull or push to happen. You can feel the sudden, lurching pull of these magnetic fields when you bring a fridge magnet close to the fridge door. Once it gets close enough, the fields pull hard, and the magnet sticks to the metal with a snap!

**Do only *some* things have magnetic fields, then? Is that why magnets only work on some objects?**

Actually, since all materials contain charged particles, more or less **everything** has a magnetic field. But they do not all show obvious magnetic effects (or **properties**). This is because in most materials, the chaotic spins and motions of their particles create two or more magnetic fields which **point in different directions,** and **cancel each other out**.

The result is a very weak magnetic field, which (if anything) **repels** other objects a bit. **Wood**, **stone**, and **plastic** typically act like this. Which is why magnets have little or no effect on them.

But a *few* types of material – such as **iron** and **cobalt** – have particles that spin and move the same way, which **aligns** all their fields in the same direction. When this happens, you get one, big magnetic field with two ends (or **poles**) where the field seems strongest. The Earth's magnetic field is focused at its north and south poles. But small, metal magnets have north and south poles, too.

Depending on how you bring them together, the poles of two different magnets will either push (repel) or pull (attract) each other. **Opposite poles** (one north, one south) will **attract** each other. But **similar poles** (two north, or two south) will **repel** each other.

## So how do you make a magnet?

Some magnetic metals and materials – like **iron**, **nickel**, and **cobalt** – are found naturally, in certain types of rock. We just dig them up, smash off the non-magnetic bits, and make them into handy shapes like bars, discs, or horseshoes.

Other metals – like **platinum**, **tungsten,** and **aluminium** – become temporarily **magnetized** (or *made* to behave like magnets) when placed in strong magnetic fields. These are the metals that strong magnets will stick to, while not really acting like strong magnets themselves.

We can also make **powerful,** temporary magnets – called **electromagnets** – by coiling metal wire around a solid chunk of iron. When you run a current through the wire, the charged particles create a strong magnetic field with two powerful magnetic poles.

**Electromagnets** are super useful because:

a) you can switch them on or off at the flick of an electric switch, and
b) you can reverse the direction of the current to make them **repel** things, rather than **attract** them.

With these two simple functions, you can do some pretty cool things.

## Like what?

You can build **electric motors**, for starters. The electric motors used in **robot arms**, **conveyer belts** and **electric cars** are all based on electromagnets. If you place one electromagnet between two regular magnets with opposing poles, then it will repel first one pole, and then the other – spinning in place hundreds or thousands of times per second. Attach that spinning electromagnet to some wheels or gears and boom – instant magno-power.

Electromagnets can also be placed in trains and tracks to create **maglev** (**magnetic levitation**) trains. These are trains that float above their tracks, held up by the repulsion of powerful electromagnets, and driven forward at speeds of over **360 mph (580 km/h)** by rapidly switching the current (and poles) of the electromagnets in the tracks.

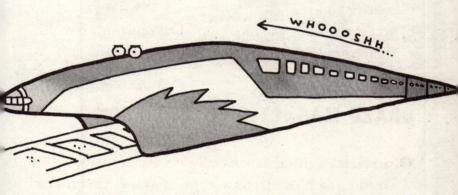

Maglev trains already exist in China and Japan. And right now, several countries are working to create **Hyperloop** maglev trains that race through under-ground tunnels at over **760 mph (12,000 km/h)** – faster than most passenger planes!

**Whoa! That would be pretty awesome! Might have to wear a seat belt, though. Wouldn't want to fly out of my seat at 700 miles an hour.**

Yeah. That would probably hurt.

# CRAZY MAGNETIC FUTURE TECH

- In 2015, Central Japan Railways broke a new speed record with their prototype **maglev (magnetic levitation) train**, when it hit **374 mph (600 km/h)** on a test track near Mount Fuji. That's about *twice* as fast as the high-speed Eurostar train that races from London to mainland Europe.

- Also in 2015, the luxury car company Lexus built a prototype **hoverboard** with magnetic levitation technology. The board floats **3 cm (1 inch)** above a metal skateboard ramp, and you can glide, drift, and pull turns without ever touching the ground. Unfortunately, it will not work on regular concrete roads and pavements. But they're working on it.

- A team of engineers in the USA is currently working on **magnetic 'repulsor helmets'** for American Football players. The idea is to cut down on the damage done when players' heads collide, by placing lightweight magnets inside the helmets that repel others at close distances.

- Google, Tesla, Volvo, and several other companies are working on **self-driving cars** that sense magnets' place in the road and use them to navigate between cities. While some cars already have self-driving systems, no magnetic roads have been built just yet.

- NASA and other space agencies once thought about using maglev technology to launch shuttles into space. This would mean building an immense tube lined with electromagnets to accelerate a shuttle skyward at over **25,000 mph (40,000 km/h)** – the speed needed to get it into orbit. The idea is probably too expensive, and it's not clear who would volunteer to be shot out of this massive **magnetic cannon**!

# WHY ARE SOME SOUNDS LOUDER THAN OTHERS?

Sounds are actually waves of pressure moving through air, water, or solid objects. They are created when solid objects wobble and vibrate the air around them. The stronger the vibration, the bigger the wave, and the louder the sound.

**Sounds are waves? I thought you could only make waves in water.**

Nope – you can make waves in almost anything. They are just much easier to see in water than they are in gases or solid objects. **Air** is a mixture of **invisible gases** (mostly oxygen and nitrogen), so you can't really see waves moving through it – you can only feel them. Solid objects like **tables**, **forks**, and **dinner plates** vibrate hard when you hit them. But the movement is so small and quick that it is impossible for our eyes to see.

Regardless, when a spoon is banged against a dinner plate, the collision makes both objects vibrate, and sends invisible ripples through the air.

## Which way does the wave go?

*Every* way. Like a pebble tossed into a pond, the ripples (or soundwaves) **spread out in all directions**. From there, they might **bounce** off walls and ceilings, be **scattered** or **absorbed** by a soft, fuzzy carpet, or **slip right into an earhole**. All of this happens pretty fast. Soundwaves pass through the air at around **760 mph (1,200 km/h)**. And very quickly, the spoon (and the plate) will stop vibrating, having passed all their energy to the air. With the source of the waves now gone, the sound quickly **decays**, or dies out.

Some objects – like **metal bells** and **guitar strings** – vibrate much better and longer than others. So the sounds created when they vibrate can **ring out** for longer before they start to decay. Many **musical instruments** are designed to create larger and longer vibrations, so that their sounds can be sustained for longer. (Except for drums and percussion instruments, that is – which are designed to make **quick, loud bangs and crashes** in a regular rhythm).

## So what happens if you hit the plate again, after the sound has died out?

If you hit the plate with the spoon *again*, then *more* soundwaves are created in the air, and another, similar sound rings out. If you hit the plate a little **harder** the second time, then the plate and spoon vibrate harder, too – producing bigger, more intense waves of pressure in the air, and **louder**, more **intense** sounds. The bigger the **vibration**, the higher the **volume**.

## But what if you hit the table with the spoon instead? Why does that make a different kind of sound?

Because depending on their size, shape, and what they are made of, different objects vibrate at different **speeds**, or **frequencies**. Plates are made of stone, plastic, or glass. When you hit the plate **harder**, you create **larger** ripples in the air – but the **number of ripples per second** stays the same. But if you hit the large, wooden table instead, then the number of ripples per second will change. In this case, there will be **fewer** ripples per second, creating a **lower, deeper** sound.

Every object vibrates in its own way, creating its own, unique sound. This is why *clanging bells* sound different from *thudding* tabletops. This is also why **violins** sound different from **pianos**, and why **pianos** sound different from **trumpets**:

- **Violins** have small, hollow bodies, and their strings are vibrated by the dragging of a hairy bow across them. The strings make the whole body of the violin vibrate, and the waves that emerge from its s-shaped sound-holes are high-speed (or high-frequency) ones, creating a recognizable *zing* (or screech, depending on how bad you are at playing violin).

- **Pianos** have large, hollow bodies, containing 88 strings, connected to a couple of hundred strings with little hammers suspended above them. When you hit a piano key, the hammer drops on the string, making the string vibrate. Different keys drop different hammers, and each of the 88 strings is tightened (or tuned) so that they vibrate at different **frequencies** – some higher, others lower. But all of them have that deep, mellow *plonk* sound that you recognize as 'piano-like'.

- **Trumpets** are not only shaped differently, they are also made of metal, rather than wood. The vibration in a trumpet is created when you blow air through your lips, making them buzz, flap, and vibrate close to the trumpet's mouthpiece. This creates a vibrating **column of air** inside the tubes of the trumpet, which race through and emerge from the open end with a satisfying *parp*.

**Hahaha! Okay, here's one – why do farts sound like trumpets, then?**

Same idea, only with the vibrating 'lips' at the other end of the tube. Toots are made when you push air (stinky waste gases produced during digestion) out of your tubular guts, or intestines. At the exit (the anus), there is a muscle called the **sphincter**, which snaps shut to keep those gases (and other things) from dribbling out of your bottom all day long. When you squeeze out a fart, the gases rush past the sphincter, which **snaps and vibrates** in the stinky wind.

Depending on how hard you push – and how tight those sphincter muscles are – the result can be anything from 'raspy kazoo' to 'pleasing bum trumpet' to 'deep trouser tuba'.

## Hahahhahahahaha! Brilliant!

Science: never boring, if you ask the right questions.

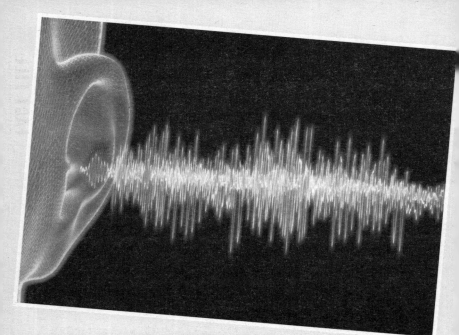

# THE SCIENCE OF NOISE

● The **loudness** of sounds is measured on the **decibel** (dB) scale, which goes from **0** (close to silence) to **120** (painfully loud) and beyond. On this scale, a **bee buzzing** in a small room would score **20** decibels, while a **gun-shot** in the same room would score **120** decibels.

● Human ears are more sensitive to **quiet, low-volume** sounds than they are to **louder** ones. This is largely because the ability to hear quiet sounds – like a trickle of water far away in the forest, or the snap of a twig as someone sneaks up on you – was more useful to our ancestors than the ability to sense just how loud that last thunderclap was.

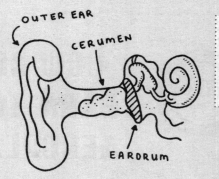

- The **scientific study of sounds** is called **acoustics.**

- **There are no sounds in space,** because there are no molecules to carry soundwaves through it. So all those rocket engine noises and explosions in sci-fi movies would actually be silent (but a lot less fun to watch).

- **Whale songs** can travel over **500 miles (800 km)** underwater. Biologists think they can navigate and meet across entire oceans by singing.

- The **loudest naturally ocurring sound** on Earth is an **erupting volcano.** When the Krakatoa volcano in Indonesia erupted in 1883, it made the loudest sound in human history. It was measured at 172 decibels over **100 miles** away, and could be *heard* over **3,000** miles away.

# HOW DID WE LEARN TO MAKE AEROPLANES?

Watching birds fly and copying their wing shapes got us started, and led us to build the first gliders around 200 years ago. But modern aeroplanes never really took off until we added engines in 1903. That turned fancy, controlled falling into proper, powered flight. Overcoming gravity is hard, and it took us a long time to figure out how to do it.

'Took off'. Ha, ha. I see what you did there.

Heh, heh.

So why did it take us so long? We've been building floaty boats and ships for ages, right? Why did aeroplanes take us so much longer?

Flying is hard, because **unsupported objects** – whether they are feathers, bowling balls, or aeroplanes – **tend to fall quickly to Earth**, thanks to **gravity**. Gravity is a **fundamental force** of the universe that **pulls objects towards each other**.

Remember when we talked about **magnets** and **magnetic fields**? Well, gravity works a bit like that. Only it acts on *everything* – not just magnetized metals and materials. In any case – the more massive the object, the stronger its **gravitational field**, and the more powerful its pull on other objects is.

From our perspective here on Earth, the **planet** is by far the most massive object around. So everything else is held tight to the planet by the pull of its gravitational field. This includes our **oceans**, our **atmosphere**, our **forests**, our **buildings**, and **ourselves**. When we try to leave the Earth's surface, however briefly, it pulls us back towards its centre, making us **drop** or **sink** down until we hit solid ground again.

**But boats don't sink. They float on the surface of the water.**

That is true. A floating boat balances the downward pull of gravity with another force, called **upthrust**. This is the upward pressure that a liquid or gas applies on an object that floats in it. You can think of it as the **floating force.** On water, we call this force **buoyancy**. In the air, we call it **lift**.

But for an object to float – whether it is a raft on the ocean or a balloon in the sky – it has to **weigh less** than the volume of air or water it displaces. A **wooden** raft will **float** because it weighs less than the volume of water it is pushing out of the way as it sits in the water. But a solid iron raft with the same size and shape will **sink**, as it is heavier than that same volume of water. In the wooden raft, **upthrust (or lift) balances gravity**, so it stays afloat. In the iron raft, gravity overcomes upthrust, and it sinks.

**Hang on – some wooden ships are enormous. And massive battleships are built out of metal, aren't they?**

Ah, but those ships are **hollow**, and mostly filled with air. As long as the whole ship (plus its crew, its cargo, and the volume of air inside it) still weighs less than the water its hollow hull displaces, then it will still float – even if it weighs **50,000 tonnes** or more (as many battleships and oil tankers do). Believe it or not, that is still less than a battleship-sized volume of water would weigh.

## Hmmm. Okay – I think I get it.

In fact, the first true **aircraft** used this 'lighter-than' idea to float a basket full of people into the sky. **Hot air balloons** are filled with heated air, which is thinner and lighter than the cooler air of the surrounding atmosphere. If a balloon, its hot air, and the basket full of people attached to it weigh less than the volume of air it occupies, then the pressure of the air around it will create enough **lift** to counteract gravity, lifting the balloon high into the sky.

In 1783, two French bothers – **Joseph and Etienne Montgolfier** – used this idea to fly over Paris in the first, manned, hot-air balloon. A couple of years later, two balloonists flew one over the English Channel.

## Yeah, but balloons are pretty rubbish, aren't they? I mean, they're really slow, and they only go where the wind blows them.

Right. To get anywhere fast, or to move against the wind, you need to create another force that **drives your vehicle forwards**. We call this force **thrust**.

Ships got around this problem at first by adding **movable sails**, and positioning them so that wind hitting the sail would drive the ship forwards, in the general direction they wanted to go. Later, we added **propellers** driven by **steam engines**. These propellers used energy from steam to drive a huge propeller wheel, pushing water backwards and the ship forwards.

## So why couldn't we just put steam engines on an aeroplane?

Well, we tried. But alas, **steam planes** were not to be. After **gliders** were invented in the late 1890s, people soon realized that a glider – especially a heavy one with people in it – cannot fight gravity for long. So to keep a heavy, manned aircraft in the air, you would need something like a boat propeller to drive it forwards.

To keep a powered aircraft in the air, you have to generate enough forward motion (or **thrust**) to send a rush of air over and around the wings. If the speed of that moving air is high enough, then the wing's shape will produce a large difference in pressure above and below the wing, creating lift. In short, to overcome gravity in a powered aircraft, you need lots of **thrust**, and lots of **speed**.

## And steam engines aren't powerful enough for that?

Well, you can build very powerful steam engines. And in theory, you could build one powerful enough to get a small aircraft to 60 mph (100 km/h), which is enough to get one off the ground. After all, steam trains have been going faster than that for over a century. But the sheer mass of a steam engine (plus the heavy coal used to fuel them) makes them very heavy. Put one of those in an **aircraft**, and you will not have a lightweight glider any more. You will have a highly effective **plummeting machine**.

For fast, reliable, powered flight, we had to wait until **petrol- or gas-powered engines** came along. **Internal combustion engines** were invented in 1872. But it took about **30 years** before two American engineers, **Orville and Wilbur Wright,** thought of attaching one to their unique biplane glider. In **December 1903**, the brothers flew their wood-framed, petrol-powered *Wright Flyer* a distance of **4 miles (6 km)** over Kitty Hawk, North

Carolina, USA. With that, the age of aeroplanes had truly begun.

Since then, more or less every fixed-wing aircraft we have built – from passenger airliners to jet fighters – follows the same basic idea and design.

**But jet fighters don't look anything like biplanes. Jet fighters look more like missiles, and biplanes look like boxes with wings.**

Ah – that's because there is one more force we haven't talked about. It's called **air resistance**, or **drag**.

**Drag** comes from trillions of air molecules pulling and dragging at the solid surface of the aircraft, like a trillion tiny magnets*. As the aircraft speeds up and air rushes under, over, and around it, its **lift** increases – but so does its **drag**. To get around this, we make our aircraft into more and more aerodynamic shapes that cut through the air more easily. This decreases drag, and allows the aircraft to reach higher and higher speeds with the same engine thrust. With these improved designs, jet airliners can easily cruise at over **600 mph (1000 km/h)**, and jet fighters can reach **3,000 mph (4,800 km/h)** or more.

........................................................................................

* Ships experience drag, too. Their motion through the water is slowed by the drag (or **water resistance**) of water molecules against their hulls.

Once you understand these four basic forces of **aerodynamics** – **gravity**, **lift**, **thrust**, and **drag** – you can invent all kinds of interesting solutions to the problem. Including **paragliders**, **helicopters**, **jet packs**, and **spaceplanes**.

Whooosh

## Wait – jet packs are *real*?

Yup. They're real, and they work. They fly at 60 mph (100 km/h), and in theory they can reach altitudes of over 3 miles (5,000 m). But sadly, they only fly for about 10 minutes at a time before running out of fuel.

## Don't care. Want one.

They also cost about £190,000 (**$250,000**). Better start saving . . .

## ALL ABOUT AIRCRAFTS

- The **Sikorsky X-Wing** was built in the 1980s, and combines jet engines and aeroplane wings with massive helicopter rotors. Sadly, it was scrapped in 1988.

- A tyre maker called Goodyear once built an inflatable aeroplane for the US Army, called the **Inflatoplane**. It worked, but the Army decided that having an aeroplane that could be popped like a balloon probably wasn't a great idea.

- The massive **Boeing 787 Dreamliner** holds over 280 passengers, and weighs 253,000 kg (250 tons). It can also fly for over 5 hours with only one engine working.

- **Concorde** was a supersonic (faster-than-sound) jet airliner that flew between Europe and the United States from 1976 to 2003. It could travel at 1,354 mph (2,180 km/h), and get from New York to London in a little under **three hours** – about twice as fast as most modern airliners.

- At any given time, there are over **8,000** aeroplanes in the air, worldwide.

# TRY IT YOURSELF:
# SINKING AND FLOATING

Gather 8–10 household items of various weights and materials. Here are some ideas: balls, balloons, sticks, shoes, paperclips, oranges (skin on), oranges (skin off).

Make a hypothesis (or theory) about which items will sink in water and which will float. For each one, ask yourself: *Why* would it sink? *Why* would it float?

Fill a large bowl with water, and one at a time, test each item to see whether it floats or sinks.

Record your findings, and if the results were unexpected, think about why objects sank when you thought they would float, or vice versa. Eureka! You just ran a complete scientific experiment!

Balls

Sticks

Balloons

Paperclips

Shoes

skin-on & skin-off

Oranges

FUN

# WHY ARE SOME THINGS GASES AND OTHERS ARE LIQUIDS?

Most chemicals and materials can exist as solids, liquids, *and* gases. But depending on the kinds of atoms they are made of – and how those atoms are bound together – they turn from solids to liquids and gases at different temperatures and pressures. So the liquids and gases we see all around us only look and behave that way right now. When they get hotter or colder, they can change their chemical state very quickly.

**So everything is made of atoms?**

Yep – every kind of matter. From the air you breathe to the ground you stand on. From acorns to aircraft carriers. From gold nuggets to poo nuggets . . .

**Okay, okay – I get the idea. So why doesn't everything look and feel the same?**

Atoms are like the **Lego bricks** of the universe. And just like Lego bricks, they come in a wide range of **types** and **sizes**, which can be combined to build more or less anything.

Each unique kind of atom is called an **element**. There are over **118** different atom types (or elements) – each one with its own unique qualities or **properties**.

Some elements – like **oxygen**, **sodium**, and **aluminium** – are **highly reactive**. They ignite or explode more easily, and they love to combine with other elements to form new shapes.

Other elements – like **helium**, **neon**, and **argon** – are the exact opposite. They are **non-reactive** by nature, and do not combine with other elements much at all.

When elements *do* combine, they form **molecules**. These can be as small and simple as a **hydrogen gas molecule ($H_2$)** – which is just two hydrogen atoms stuck together.

Add an **oxygen atom** to that, and you get two hydrogen atoms stuck to one oxygen atom – which is **water** (or $H_2O$). Smash that together with some extra **carbon** and **oxygen** atoms and you end up with a **vitamin C molecule** ($C_6H_8O_6$) – which contains **six**

**carbon** atoms, **six oxygen** atoms, and **eight hydrogen** atoms.

Obviously, **hydrogen**, **water**, and **vitamin C** are all very different things. In their most familiar forms, hydrogen is a **gas**, water is a **liquid**, and vitamin C is a **solid**. But they are all made from elements combined in various ways to make new chemical substances. And interestingly, they can change their chemical **state** from solid to liquid, or from liquid to gas, while keeping their identities. Water, for example, can be a liquid (**water**), a solid (**ice**) or a gas (**water vapour**, or **steam**). Liquid water, ice, and water vapour are three different **states** of the same substance. It just takes on different shapes and behaviours at different temperatures.

**So why do they do that?**

It's all to do with how their molecules are bound together. When you throw a bunch of water ($H_2O$) molecules together at room temperature, they will bind loosely together into a **liquid**.

In a **liquid**, the molecules can move and flow around each other, but rarely separate altogether. With their molecules held together this way, liquids can **change their shape** to fit the container you pour them into, but they will keep the **same volume**.

Now if you add heat to liquid water, you start to break the loose bonds between the water molecules. The ones at the edges (or surface) will separate from the pack and drift away as molecules of water vapour. Add enough heat, and all the liquid water will turn to gas (steam). Congratulations – you have just **vaporized** (or **boiled**) the water. Boiling changes the state of a substance from liquid to **gas**.

In a **gas**, the molecules are barely held together at all. They can spread out, move apart, go more or less anywhere they want. Thanks to this freedom, gases can not only **change their shape**, they can also **change their volume** – thinning out and **expanding to fill the container** they are in completely.

**But what if you cooled it down again? Would it go back to being a liquid?**

Yep – it certainly would. As you cool (or remove heat energy) from water vapour, the gassy molecules fall together again, loosely binding into droplets of liquid water. We call this change from a gas to a liquid state **condensation**. You see it happening on windows when the cold air outside cools and turns into water vapour inside your cozy house. It also explains why swimming goggles 'mist up' (water vapour in the warm air trapped by the goggles is cooled and condensed into tiny droplets by the cold water in the pool).

## So when does water turn into ice?

If you cool liquid water down enough, then the molecules slow down, pack together, and bind more and more strongly to each other. Eventually, they form the **solid** state of water, better known as **ice.**

In a **solid**, the molecules are so tightly bound that they can **hardly move at all**. Solids cannot spread out to fill things like liquids and gases do, and tend to **keep the same shape** unless **bent**, **cut**, or **broken**. Of course, you can always add a little heat and loosen up the molecules again, turning the solid ice into liquid water once more.

We call the change of state from liquid to solid **freezing,** and the change back from solid to liquid . . .

## Melting!

Bingo. This is how one substance can shift state from solid to liquid to gas and back again[*], and

--------------------------------------------------

[*] Sometimes, things go straight from **solid to gas**, or straight from **gas to solid**. We call these **sublimation** and **deposition**. But that's not so important to know.

most substances can exist in **any one** of these states.

**So you can make liquid iron? Or solid oxygen?**

Yup. All you need is the right temperature and pressure.

Solid **iron** melts (or becomes a liquid) at around **1,500°C (2,800°F)**. Way hotter than most ovens you can get, but doable with a super-hot **forge** inside an ironworks. Making liquid iron, and pouring it into special moulds to solidify, is how we make **cast iron** objects and tools.

As for **oxygen**, it floats about as a **gas** in our warmish, low-pressure atmosphere. But if you cool it to **-183°C (-297°F)**, it turns into liquid oxygen. Liquid oxygen can be used as rocket fuel, or kept inside spacecraft, submarines, and high-altitude aircraft to create breathable oxygen gas. Liquid oxygen **freezes**, or becomes a solid, at **-218°C (-362°F)**. **Solid oxygen** crystals are hard to create, but have special magnetic and electrical properties.

solid  →(Melting) →  liquid  →(Vaporization) →  gas
solid  ←(Freezing) ←  liquid  ←(Condensation) ←  gas

**Crazy!**

You can even change the state of mixed molecules like **carbon dioxide** and **air**.

**Solid carbon dioxide** is called **dry ice**, and we use it to keep foods cool during transport, and to create dramatic smoke effects in theatres and rock concerts!

**Liquid air** is a pale blue liquid made from cooling and **condensing** normal air (a mix of oxygen, nitrogen, and other gases) to **-194°C (-317°F)**. We use liquid air to cool and condense other gases – like neon and xenon, used in electrical lighting.

**Okay – one more question. Can you make liquid ice cream?**

Err – that's easy. Just eat it verrrrrrrrry slowly.

# QUICK ONES –
# ELEMENTS AND CHEMISTRY

**How do elements get their names?**

Some elements – like **silver**, **gold**, and **lead** – were named in ancient times and have simply kept their names. Others are named after **planets** (**uran**ium, **saturn**ium), ancient **gods** (**thor**ium, **titan**ium), famous **people** (**einstein**ium), or the **places** they were discovered (**german**ium, **francium**, **californ**ium).

The rest are named for how they behave. The famously non-reactive gas **argon**, for example, comes from the Greek word *argos*, meaning *lazy*. The pungent gas **Bromine** comes from the Greek word *bromos*, meaning *stench!*

## Where did all the different elements on Earth come from?

In short, from the heart of an exploding star! In the beginning, the universe was filled with free **hydrogen**, the simplest of all elements. When hydrogen clumps and fuses together inside **stars**, it creates **helium** (this nuclear reaction also throws off immense amounts of light and heat, which is where the energy in sunlight comes from). At the end of their lives, particularly massive stars can collapse into themselves, creating immense heat and pressure. Inside this super-hot forge, hydrogen and helium are fused to make **carbon**, **oxygen**, and all other other elements. When the star finally explodes in a violent **supernova**, those elements are blasted across space, to be drawn into orbit around new stars as **planets**, **moons**, **asteroids**, and **comets**. This is where *all* the elements on Earth, and inside every living thing on its surface, came from. In other words, **you are made of exploding star-stuff**!

## Awesome! What are diamonds made of?

Diamonds are made entirely from the element **carbon** – crushed and compressed into beautiful, clear crystals **90–150 miles (150–200 km)** beneath the ground, in the Earth's **upper mantle**. The crystals are shifted towards the crust by the movement of magma and volcanic eruptions. Diamond miners dig them out of seams of volcanic rock, in what is often difficult and dangerous work (which is partly why they are so valuable). Incredibly, diamonds are made of the same stuff as **graphite** – the stuff inside pencils. In theory, you could heat and compress a bunch of pencils to make diamonds for yourself! This can actually be done in special laboratories, creating 'artificial' diamonds. But it takes massive amounts of heat and pressure, so sadly, you probably won't be able to do it at home.

## What's the rarest metal on Earth?

You might think it is silver, or gold. But in fact, it's an extremely rare semi-metal called astatine, which is formed naturally in the Earth's crust by the decay of uranium and thorium. There are at least **250,000 tonnes** of gold on Earth, and over **2 million tonnes** of silver. But there are probably only **28 grams** (less than **1 ounce**) of astatine in the Earth's crust. This is because it spontaneously decays into lighter elements after just 8–16 hours. Its name comes from the Greek word *astatos*, meaning *unstable*.

## Are any of the elements dangerous?

Actually, quite a few of them are. **Arsenic**, **mercury**, and **thallium** are deadly **poisons**. **Fluorine** is a **corrosive gas** that burns your skin and eyeballs. **Caesium** may look like pretty, yellow gold, but it reacts with almost everything, and **explodes** if you drop it into water. **Polonium**, **plutonium**, **uranium**, and **curium** are just four of **38 radioactive elements**, which throw off deadly, cancer-causing **radiation** as they continuously decay over time. Toxicologists (scientists who study toxic substances) have a saying: 'Everything is toxic in a high enough dose'. But unless you are a trained scientist, some elements should be avoided altogether!

# BLOOD, GUTS, AND POO

# DOES THE HEART MAKE BLOOD?

The heart does not actually make blood – it just moves your blood around. It forms the central part of your circulatory system, which delivers heat, oxygen, nutrients, hormones, and antibodies throughout the human body, and clears away waste materials. But blood itself is made elsewhere.

**So where *is* blood made?**

Blood is actually made in your **bones**. Specifically, in **bone marrow**, which is a kind of spongy tissue found inside your bones.

## I thought bones were hard and empty!

Only when you remove them from the body. **Living** bones are hard, chalky tubes with soft, spongy centres*. Packed inside are millions of living cells, which make – among other things – new **bone tissue** and fresh **blood cells**. These blood cells leave the bones via **blood vessels** (more on those in a minute) that run through the marrow, and through tiny holes in the bone itself.

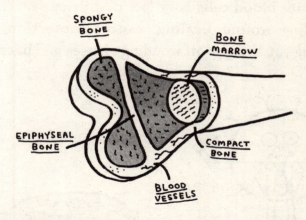

SPONGY BONE

BONE MARROW

EPIPHYSEAL BONE

COMPACT BONE

BLOOD VESSELS

## What's blood actually made of? I mean, what's in it?

Blood is a mixture of four things: **plasma**, **platelets**, **red blood cells**, and **white blood cells**. **Plasma** is mostly

* This is the bit your dog likes to lick clean after cracking a bone into pieces. Apparently it's delicious.

water – which is one reason why we have to drink so much of it – with certain salts and proteins dissolved in it. Plasma forms the wet, liquid base that holds all the other stuff you find in blood. **Platelets** are tiny cells that clump together to stop bleeding when you are injured, by forming solid **clots** and **plugs**.

**Red blood cells** carry **oxygen** from the lungs to body tissues, and the waste-gas **carbon dioxide** back from the body to the lungs.

**White blood cells** have lots of different functions, including **wound healing**, **cancer protection**, and helping you to **fight off** invading **viruses** and **bacteria**.

**Why do you need so many different kinds of blood cells?**

Because each type of cell does a different job. All **platelets** need to do is sense an injury and clump together. **Red blood cells** are basically just delivery guys – carrying oxygen and carbon dioxide back and forth using a special, iron-based **haemoglobin** protein trapped inside. But **white blood cells** perform far more complex and interesting tasks, so they come in all shapes and sizes. To **haematologists** (doctors and scientists who study blood), they even have different names. **Phagocytes** ('cell-munchers') **target and destroy** invading bacteria, engulfing them and digesting them using special digestive enzymes. **Lymphocytes,** meanwhile, are super-clever cells that **communicate** and **co-ordinate** their attacks on invading microbes and infected cells, and allow the body to **remember** and **recognize** previous invaders. So it is these cells that give us **immunity** to viruses and bacteria.

**Got it. So why do we need so much blood in our bodies? I mean, don't you pass out, or even die, if you lose too much of it?**

That's true – you do. That is because our brains and internal organs are hungry things. They need a constant supply of **energy** from the food we eat, and a constant supply of **oxygen** in order to release that energy and put it to work. If we cannot get that energy and oxygen to our brains, muscles, and other organs, then they stop working and we pass out, fall down, and (eventually) die.

Some simple sea creatures like **jellyfish** and **sponges** do not really need **blood** or a **circulatory system**, as everything they need just drifts (or **diffuses**) in and out of their bodies, and in and out of the simple **organs** inside.

But large, complex animals like **sharks**, **snakes**, **rats**, **monkeys**, and **humans** are different. We have highly complex bodies, stuffed with highly **complex organs**, doing very different jobs. Water, oxygen, and nutrients do not just drift into our bodies from the air or water around us. We have to **swallow and suck them in**, **move them efficiently** to our brains, muscles and organs, **gather the waste products** they create, and **pump them back out again** somehow. That is what blood – and the circulatory system – is for.

This is how the whole system breaks down:

## Blood

Blood is the first and most important part of that system, as it holds and transports the **oxygen** and **nutrients** themselves. Blood also carries energy in the form of **heat**. It is warmed up as it passes through heat-generating tissues, and carries that heat throughout the body, keeping us warm all over. And as we have already learned, the cells inside can help protect us from injures, infections, and more.

## Blood Vessels

But to get where it needs to go, blood has to move through **tubes**, also known as **blood vessels**. These vessels are organized like the trunk and branches of a tree.

Wide, trunk-like **arteries** carry blood from the heart up to the brain, out to the lungs and arms, and down to the legs and abdominal organs. Wide, trunk-like **veins** carry blood back to the heart and lungs to dump waste materials and get resupplied with fresh oxygen. In between, the arteries and veins split and divide into thinner branches called **arterioles** and **venules**, and divide again close to the organs (within your skin) into super-thin **capillaries**. Together, the blood vessels channel everything where it needs to be, and back again.

## Heart

Last, but by no means least, you have the **heart**. Without a heart, blood would not move through your blood vessels – it would just sit there like a stuck train, unable to carry anything anywhere. The heart is a **muscular pump** that pushes blood through the whole network of blood vessels. It has to pump constantly from the day you are born\*, and never gets a day off. If the heart stops beating – even for a minute – you have serious problems, as you cannot get oxygen to the brain. Without enough oxygen, the brain can be damaged or stop working altogether. This is called a **heart attack**, and when it happens, doctors have to try to restart the heart as soon as possible.

**Wow. That sounds pretty scary.**

Right. Which is one reason why you should look after your heart – and the rest of your circulatory system – by eating the **right foods**, and getting plenty of **exercise**. Eating too many sugary, fatty foods can leave too much **fat** in your blood, which sticks to the walls of your blood vessels and **clogs** them up. This makes it harder

......................................................................

\* Actually, a lot earlier than that. Your heart starts beating about 8 months *before* you a born, while you are still just a month-old foetus inside your mother's tummy!

214

for the heart to pump the blood around, and it strains and struggles to do so. And if you never get outside and exercise, your heart and lungs become weaker, putting more strain on them both when you eventually *do* have to move around. This makes heart attacks more likely.

On the flipside, eating **healthy, whole foods** (especially plant-based ones) and **exercising regularly** can help keep your fat levels low, your blood vessels clean, and your heart and lungs good and strong.

**Right – I'm off for a veggie snack and a bike ride.**

Good idea. Happy heart, happy life!

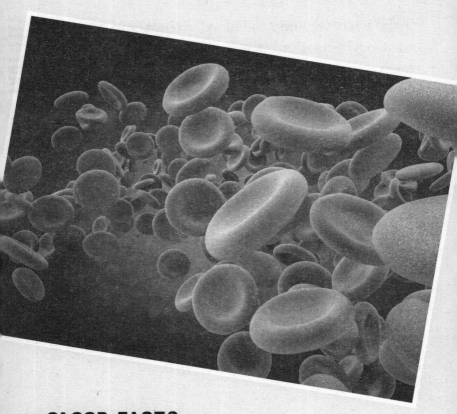

# BLOOD FACTS

● An adult human's body contains about **5 litres** (10 pints, or 1.3 gallons) of blood.

● Blood makes up about 8% of your total body weight. So if you weigh **20 kg (45 lb)**, then about **1.6 kg (3.6 lb)** of that is blood alone.

- Different types of **blood cells** have different lifespans. **Red blood cells** hang around for 4 months before being recycled, while **white blood cells** only last a few hours or days.

- Human blood is **red** because it is thick with red blood cells. Red blood cells contain an iron-rich protein called **haemoglobin**, which reflects red light.

- Many insects have pale **yellow** blood, while crabs, spiders and octopuses have **blue** blood. Some worms and leeches have **green** or **violet** blood.

- There are eight major **blood types**: O⁺, O⁻, A⁺, A⁻, B⁺, B⁻, AB⁺ and AB⁻. Some blood types do not mix well, and attack each other when mixed. This means it is important to know your blood type before giving or receiving blood. The most common blood types vary a lot from country to country, but worldwide, **O⁺, A⁺, and B⁺** are by far the most common.

- The rarest is **AB⁻**.

(Mine is **B⁺**, or **B-positive**. Which also happens to be my motto.)

# COULD WE STILL MOVE AROUND IF WE DIDN'T HAVE BONES?

We could – but not very well, and it wouldn't look pretty. Though some animals make do without them, reptiles, mammals, and other vertebrate animals use bones to create almost all of our movements – from walking and crawling to jumping, running, and swimming. But it takes more than just bones and muscles to move like we do. It also takes *brains*.

**But do we really *need* bones to move? Couldn't we just use our muscles instead?**

Well, **muscles** *are* the basic motors of most animal bodies, including ours. And some animals, like **earthworms** and **jellyfish**, can get around without bones by squeezing, rippling, and pulsing different parts of their squishy bodies, creating **waves** (or **undulations**) of muscle tension that move them through the ground, or through the water.

But worms and jellyfish aren't exactly the best movers on the planet*. If you want to speed up, slow down, or change direction quickly, then you need **bones** to do it. Bones give you something to **anchor your muscles** to, and **stiff**, **solid limbs** you can use to **walk**, **crawl**, or **paddle**.

## So which were the first animals to grow bones?

As far as we know, **fish** were the first bony animals. Not *all* fish have bones. The earliest known fish species had no bones at all, and some (like stingrays and manta rays) *still* don't. But one group – imaginatively called **bony fish** – developed bony spines and fins around **400 million** years ago. Bony fish were **faster** and **more powerful** than their non-bony cousins, and soon came to dominate the oceans.

A short while later (well, about 10 million years later) **bony fish** had evolved into bony **tetrapods.** These four-legged **creatures** flopped and crawled out of the oceans

---

* Which is why they are easily nabbed and eaten by birds and sea turtles, respectively.

219

to colonize the land during the **Devonian** period. Eventually, these guys would evolve into **amphibians** (frogs, newts, and salamanders) and **reptiles** (snakes, lizards, and dinosaurs) – animal types that are still with us today.

As they adapted to life on land, **amphibians** and **reptiles** used their bony limbs and spines to **flop**, **hop**, **slither**, and **crawl** their way around the planet. A few even mastered **walking** and **running** – notably the theropod dinosaurs like *Velociraptor* and *Tyrannosaurus rex*. Thanks to their bone-powered movement, these strong, agile reptiles ruled the land for over **200 million years**.

**So what happened then?**

*We* did. From **rats** and **shrews** to **cats**, **horses**, and **kangaroos** – we hairy, bony **mammals** are the *true* masters of complex movement. While frogs can hop, and reptiles can crawl, slither and scuttle, mammals can do *soooo* much more.

Mammals can **walk**, **crawl**, **trot**, **run**, **leap**, **jump**, **climb**, **swing**, **stalk**, **pounce** . . . the list of movements is almost endless. It is probably no accident that we mammals came to replace the reptiles as the dominant, bony animals on the planet. Or that the dinosaurs only managed to survive by taking to the skies as bony, fast-moving birds. We pretty much **outran**, **outhunted**, and **out-manoeuvred** every other large animal within a few million years.

Now, 66 million years later, we bony **humans** are the dominant mammals on the planet. And we are probably the best movers of all. With our balanced, upright stance and our clever, bony fingers, we humans can **push**, **pull**, **throw**, **catch**, **weave nets**, **craft objects**, **build shelters**, and **use weapons**. None of that would have been possible without **bones**.

**Couldn't we do *any* of those things without bones? I mean, couldn't we at least slither around like a snake or something?**

We could maybe roll, flop, and slither a little. But without bones, we could not hope to move as gracefully as a snake. Remember – snakes use bones, too – they use their long, flexible spines and ribs to create their powerful slithering motions. A snake with no bones would be a floppy, awkward mess.

**So what happens if you break a bone? That can happen, right?**

It can, and it does. Children and adults break bones all the time, often as a result of slipping, falling, or tumbling from a bike or skateboard.

Breaking a **leg** or **ankle** can leave you unable to walk for several months. Breaking an **arm** or **wrist** can make some movements awkward, but you can generally work around it until the bone heals up. Breaking your **back** or **neck** is a *lot* more serious, as your hollow **spine** (backbone and neck bones) contains the **spinal cord** – which sends signals between your brain, arms, and legs. Damage *that*, and you risk not being able to move much at all.

But other than that, you should be fine. Most broken bones heal within a couple of months.

So as long as you don't **re-break** them while they are healing – or break **all your bones at once** – then you can usually still find a way to move around with broken bones. Even if that means using **crutches** or a **walking stick** for a little while.

**Bet it's not fun, though.**

No, it's not. Broken bones **hurt**, and waiting for them to heal up (while your friends still run and play) can be very, very boring and frustrating. Which is why you should always wear pads and a helmet when you are **cycling** or **skateboarding,** and take care when **climbing trees**, or attempting new **parkour tricks**.

**Pads. Helmet. Careful. Got it.**

Good! Now crawl, trot, or run outside and play – those bones were meant for moving!

# DEM BONES, DEM BONES . . .

- **Babies have more bones than adults**. Human babies are born with around **300** bones (some made of soft cartilage, rather than solid bone). These fuse together and solidify within a few weeks, months, or years so that an adult human only has about **206.**

- **Half the bones in your body are in your hands and feet**. Each hand contains 27 bones, and each foot has 28, making 110 bones altogether.

- **The smallest bones in your body are in your ear**. The *malleus* (hammer), *incus* (anvil) and *stapes* (stirrup) are tiny bones that help you amplify sound, bridging the gap between your eardrum and the fluid-filled **cochlea** of the inner ear.

- **Doctors have known how to treat broken bones for at least 3,000 years**. Ancient Egyptian scrolls describe doctors realigning bones and wrapping them with linen bandages.

- **Bones are stronger than steel**. A bridge made of solid bone would – in theory – hold more weight than a steel one.

**You grow a new skeleton once every 10–13 years.** Bone is living tissue, and is constantly replacing itself. Different bones wear out and rebuild at different speeds. But after 10–13 years, your whole skeleton has been replaced. So if you're 10 or older, you've already regrown your skeleton at least once.

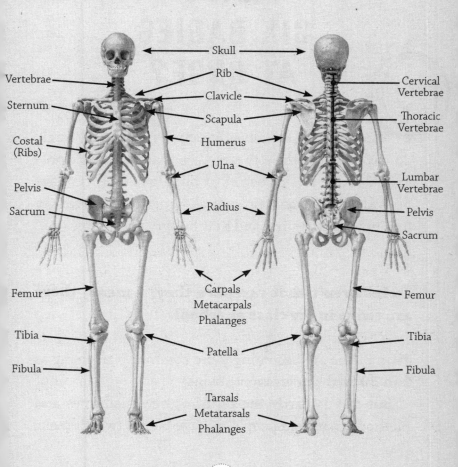

Skull

Vertebrae

Rib

Sternum

Clavicle

Scapula

Costal (Ribs)

Humerus

Ulna

Pelvis

Radius

Sacrum

Cervical Vertebrae

Thoracic Vertebrae

Lumbar Vertebrae

Pelvis

Sacrum

Femur

Carpals
Metacarpals
Phalanges

Femur

Tibia

Patella

Tibia

Fibula

Fibula

Tarsals
Metatarsals
Phalanges

# WHY DON'T HUMANS HAVE SIX BABIES AT ONCE?

We *can* have six babies at once – but we very rarely do. Even twins are pretty rare, as human births go. Some animals have lots of babies at once, while others have only one or two at a time. It all depends on how they live, how big they are, and how hungry their babies get!

**Twins aren't that rare, are they? I mean, there are twins in my class at school.**

Twin births are becoming more common – as many as **1 in 30** births now involve twins.

But this is partly the result of new medicines and methods that help people to have babies (which make twins more likely). But naturally, only **1 in 250** births result in twins.

Having **triplets** (three babies at once) is even rarer. Only **1 in 1,000** births result in triplets. As for **quadruplets**, **quintuplets** (**four** or **five** babies at once), that only happens once in every **50–100 million** births.

## What about having *six* babies at once?

Those are called **sextuplets,** and that has only happened a handful of times that we know of. Incredibly, there have even been one or two cases of **septuplets** and **octuplets** – seven or eight healthy babies, all born at once. But this almost *never* happens.

Whichever way you look at it, the simple truth is this: most of the time, in most places, in over **97%** of births – only **one** baby pops out.

## What about other animals? How many do they usually have?

Average **litter size** – or how many babies an animal usually has at once – is different from species to species. Smaller mammals like **mice**, **rats**, and **shrews** tend to have larger litters – anywhere from **six** to **twenty** babies at once. Larger mammals – like **cats**, **dogs**, and **foxes** – usually have **four** or **five** babies per litter (though **big** cats, like **lions**, **tigers**, and **leopards** often have just **two** or **three**). Primates – **lemurs**, **monkeys**, **chimpanzees**, and **gorillas** – usually have just **one** or **two** babies at a time. And the largest mammals of all – **elephants**, **rhinos**, **hippos**, and **whales** – rarely have more than **one** baby at a time.

**Why are they all different? And why do smaller animals have more babies than bigger ones?**

Good question. While not *all* small animals have large litters, and not *all* big animals have small litters\*, many animals do seem to show that pattern. This is probably because smaller animals tend to spend life on the run, hunted by larger creatures, scampering and scrounging food where they can. If your environment is dangerous, and you are not sure all your babies will make it to adulthood, then it makes sense to have lots of babies in a single litter. That way, at least one or two of them will likely survive.

Female **salmon** lay *thousands* of eggs, yet only a few will survive to a fishy adulthood. **Gerbils**, **hamsters**, and **mice** have anywhere from 8 to 30 pups. But again,

.........................................................................................

\* Tiny **elephant shrews** have just **one** or **two** babies per litter, while massive **wild boar** have an average of **six**.

in the wild, only a few will make it to adulthood. Some are eaten by predators, while others simply do not get enough to eat. Life is tough for the little guys.

Larger animals – like **elephants**, **whales** and **humans** – have fewer predators and usually live in more stable, predictable environments. For us, it makes more sense to have just **one** or **two** babies, and spend more time and energy protecting them, and making sure they get all the food they need.

**But why can't we do both? Like, have lots of big babies, *and* protect and feed them all?**

Because – as your parents will tell you – feeding and protecting big babies is exhausting work! The more babies you have at once, the more food you have to find each day. A bird with **six** chicks in its nest has to find *twice* as many worms and insects each day, compared with another bird with only **three** chicks. We mammals make **milk** to feed our babies (or at least, the females do), made in special **mammary glands**. But a mother feeding **two** babies has to make *twice* as much milk as a mother feeding **one**. Which means she has to find and eat more food herself (as it takes more food to make more milk). If she cannot find enough food, her milk will dry up, and her babies will starve.

**Hmm. I hadn't thought of it that way.**

What's more, it takes *time* to make milk, and to refill the mammary glands. To get plenty of food into them every day, each baby will need a **teat** of its own to suckle on. If you have more babies than teats, then the babies will fight over them, and at least some babies will lose out. If that happens every time, then some babies will get fat, while others will starve. Ideally, to give the mother a chance to rest – and her teats a chance to recharge – she really needs **two teats** per baby.

For this reason, the **number of teats** a mammal has is usually **equal to its maximum litter size**, and **twice** the number of its **average** (or **ideal**) **litter size**.

For example:

**Mouse mothers** have **10 teats**. They *can* have **10 or more** pups, but their **average litter size is 5** (10 divided by 2).

**Dog mothers** have **8 or 10 teats**. They *sometimes* have **8 or 10 pups**, but usually have just **4 or 5**.

**Pig mothers** have **12 or 14 teats**. They *could* have **12 or more piglets**, but more often have **7 or 8**.

And **human mothers** have just **two teats** (or more politely, **breasts**). We *can* have **two or more** babies, but we *usually* have just the **one**. See what I mean?

**So how do human mothers do it? Y'know, if they have more than two babies?**

They usually use bottles filled with **baby formula** – which is basically **powdered cow's milk** with added sugars, fats, proteins, and vitamins.

**Oh. I guess that's easier than growing extra teats.**

Definitely. Though nothing about looking after twins or triplets is easy. Keeping them *fed* is probably the least of your problems. Getting them to *sleep* at the same time – now that will give your parents nightmares for years . . .

# COOL FACTS ABOUT TWINS

● **Identical twins have *nearly* the same DNA.** Up to 99.9% identical, according to tests.

● **Identical twins have different fingerprints.** So if one committed a crime and tried to blame the other, you could *totally* tell which one did it.

● **Twins kick and fist-bump each other in the womb.** The love and competition starts early – at just 14 weeks of age.

● **Twins are more likely to be left-handed.** 20% of twins are left handed, compared to only 10% of everyday *non*-twins.

● **Roughly 40% of twins invent their own languages.** Probably to annoy their parents.

# WHY CAN'T NEWBORN BABIES STAND OR WALK?

Because compared to most other mammals, human babies are born weak, helpless, and unable to move much at all. They have to *learn* to stand and walk, and it takes them anywhere from 8 to 18 months to do it. After that, babies continue to grow and develop into children, adolescents, and adults – getting stronger and smarter all the way.

**But why can't they just get up and walk *right* away, like baby cows, or baby deer?**

How do you mean?

**I mean, wouldn't it be easier if they could follow their parents around, instead of having to be picked up and carried all the time?**

It *would* be easier, yes. For everyone. But unfortunately, that's not how it works. For starters, human babies are born with **soft bones** and **weak, floppy muscles**. This is **helpful** during birth, as it helps babies to **squeeze** their way out of the womb without hurting their mothers (too much!) on the way[*]. But it also leaves them unable to move much once they are out in the world. Also, babies lack the ability to **control** their muscles properly, as their **brains** are not quite fully formed at birth. Strength, balance, and control all come with **practice**, and **practising** new movements will literally **change the baby's brain** – with new connections forming every day. In short, it takes **time** for bones, muscles, and brains to develop, and human babies have a lot of **growing** to do before they can pull off **standing** and **walking** – let alone **running**, **climbing**, and **swimming**.

......................................................................
[*] Even their **skulls** squash a bit on their way through the narrow birth canal, leaving their heads temporarily **cone-shaped** for days or weeks afterwards!

## How much time does it take?

Growth happens gradually, and in **stages**.

Often, we talk as if there are only three or four stages in human life and growth. First, you're a **baby**. Then, you're a **child** (or **kid**). Finally, you 'grow up' to be an **adult**. And maybe somewhere in between, you're a **teenager**. But in fact, there are several more important stages within – and in between – those ones.

Before you are a baby, you are a **foetus** – growing and developing inside your mother's womb. As a foetus, you can tumble and kick a bit (causing your mother to grumble and wee more often than usual, as you stomp on her bladder). But apart from that, you have about as much movement skill as a **jellyfish**.

At birth, you become an **infant** – a largely **helpless** baby that can lie on its back or belly, grab and shove things into its mouth, and wiggle its body like a **fish** out of water (albeit an odd, pink one with mutant arms and legs). But that's about it.

After 4–6 months, you might learn how to crawl on your belly like a **reptile**. After a few months of practice, bone growth, and muscle growth, you are crawling and shuffling on all fours, with occasional attempts to stand up on your back legs. By this point, you are finally moving like a **mammal**.

## So when do we actually start walking?

By 12–18 months, most of us will master **walking**. Well, *master* is perhaps too strong a word. Become 'wobbly, **trainee** walkers' is more like it. At this point, you are a **toddler**. The more you toddle, the stronger your bones and muscles become, and the better you become at controlling them. As your body grows, so does your **brain**. You start **speaking** whole words and sentences, **copying**, **learning**, and **predicting**. Figuring out what is **safe**, what is dangerous, and above all **where the biscuits are kept**.

Between ages 3 and 11, you enter **childhood**. As a child, you keep growing taller and stronger, and your ability to move, talk, think, and learn rockets upward. You can **run**, **jump**, **climb**, learn to **swim**, learn to **dance**, learn to play sports like **football** or **basketball**.

You go to **school**, study **languages**, make **friends**, play **sports**, learn about **relationships**, and gradually become a little more **independent** from your parents. Towards the end of this stage, the physical growth of your bones and muscles slows down a bit.

But your **brain** keeps learning and changing itself, constantly.

## Then what's next – teenager?

Right. Around age 12–14 (earlier for girls, later for boys) you become an **adolescent** (a.k.a. a teenager), having reached a crazy growth stage we call **puberty**. At puberty, your physical growth speeds up again (called a **growth spurt**), and your body starts to change all over. Muscles and bones become much stronger. Body hair appears where before there was none. You get *amazing* at moving, and (with practice) you can master more or less any kind of sport or movement. You can become highly skilled at **gymnastics**, **skateboarding**, **martial arts**, whatever you decide to try. You also start to think more about **love**, **fear**, **freedom**, **friendship**, and **what you want to do** with your life. In stops and starts, you edge towards the final stage of human growth – **adulthood**.

## So then you stop growing?

In one way, yes. But in most ways, no. The truth is, you *never* really stop growing and changing, even after becoming an **adult**.

By age 20, your bones stop getting longer, and you are about as **tall** as you are ever going to be. But depending on how often you exercise, and what kinds of exercise you do, your bones and muscles can **continue** to grow and reshape themselves **throughout life**. Many **athletes** reach their peak between 20 and 30 years of age, as strength and speed hit their maximum, and years of practising movement skills start to pay off. In **early adulthood** (in your 20s and 30s) you think more about love, work, and family – perhaps having kids of your own.

Later, in your 40s, 50s, and 60s, you reach **middle adulthood.** Here, signs of ageing start to shift. Bones and muscles continue to grow, but take longer to grow than they once did.

**Hair** keeps growing in some places (oddly, in the nose and ears), but may **thin out** or **stop growing altogether** in others (like the top of the head – especially in men).

**Skin** becomes looser, **wrinkles** start to appear around the eyes, mouth, and neck.

**Healing** slows down, and it takes longer to recover from illness or injury.

By age 70, you enter **late adulthood**. At this age – which may continue through your 80s, 90s, even in to your 100s! – **bones** become more brittle, and **muscles** become weaker and less flexible. Though you *can* stay fit, strong, and mobile well into old age, it takes a lot more work and effort to do it. Through illness, injury, or lost strength, many people become less mobile by this point, and may even need **walking frames** or **wheelchairs** to get around. Healing slows, immunity drops, and you become more susceptible to **diseases** – especially of the heart, lungs, and brain. **Diet**, **exercise**, and **medical check-ups** become more important than ever, and you need more and more help from your family to stay strong, healthy, and happy.

But by this age, you pretty much **know it all**, and you can enjoy sharing a whole lifetime of knowledge and memories with your friends and family.

**Whoa. That sounds like quite a ride.**

It is. One way or the other, life never stops moving – so neither should you. Build a strong body, learn all you can, and look after your family and friends. Do these things, and you can enjoy strong bones, a healthy brain, and a long, happy life.

But above all, remember to enjoy the trip.

# BIRTH, GROWTH, AND AGEING

- **Newborns see only in black and white**. Or rather, black, white, and shades of grey. Colour vision develops slowly over the first few months of life.

- **Your brain grows fastest between birth and 5 years old.** If your body grew as fast as your brain, you would weigh over 77 kg (170 pounds) at 1 month old. That's around as much as an average adult female!

- **Kids see better in the dark than adults**. The ability to do this decreases with age.

- **Fingernails grow twice as fast as toenails** (3 mm per month, versus 1.5 mm per month, on average).

- **Human ears and noses never stop growing.** They continue to swell and droop throughout life. This is why older people often have bigger ears and noses.

- **By the time you are 90 years old** the amount of blood pumped by your heart drops by **half**.

- **The average human eats about 35 tonnes (100,000 pounds) of food** in a single lifetime. That's the equivalent of 7 Asian elephants!

243

# WHY DO WE EAT THINGS (JUST TO POO THEM OUT AGAIN)?

We eat things to power, build, and repair our bodies. We drink things to provide a watery environment where all of that can happen. We wee and poo to get rid of the leftovers, and to keep the body in a healthy balance. When all goes well, digestion is quite an amazing thing to behold!

**Okay, I get that food gives us energy. But why do we eat and poo so *much*. I mean, couldn't we just eat less, poo less, and keep more of the food in our bodies?**

Well, if you eat less, you *do* poo less. That's true. But eating food does more than just give us **energy**. It also gives us all the **materials** we need to **build and repair**

Right. Teeth kick off the process of digestion by **slicing**, **mashing**, and **grinding** your food into a soft, squishy pulp. Younger kids have around 20 **primary** (or 'baby') teeth – 10 on the top, 10 on the bottom. Some time after age five or six, baby teeth begin to fall out, to be replaced by **32 secondary**, or **adult** teeth (16 on the top, 16 on the bottom). As you may have noticed, groups of teeth have different **shapes**, relating to the different jobs they do:

- **Incisors** (your front four teeth, top and bottom) are wide, flat blades made for slicing and cutting food.

- **Canines** (the two pointy ones outside the incisors, top and bottom) are cone-shaped spears made for grabbing and tearing chunks of food. Canine teeth are also known as **cuspids**.

- **Premolars** (the two flattish teeth outside the pointy ones on each side) are also for grabbing and tearing. Premolars are also known as **bicuspids**.

- **Molars** (your three back teeth on each side, top and bottom) are wide, flat grindstones made for crushing seeds and grinding food to a pulp before it's swallowed.

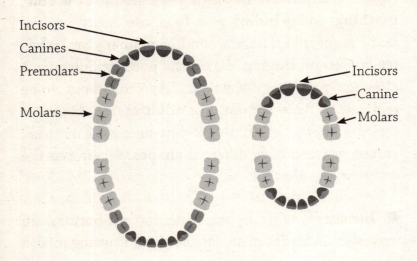

Incisors
Canines
Premolars
Molars

Incisors
Canine
Molars

Teeth are helped in this effort by the **salivary glands** – which fire juicy **saliva** (spit) into your mouth to wet the food. Saliva also contains **enzymes** that start to break down **sugars** and **starches**. When this is done, the wet wad of food (called a **bolus)** is ready to be swallowed. Know where the food goes from there?

**It goes down your food tube to your stomach.**

Correctamundo. Your food tube, or **oesophagus,** carries the food to your stomach, where it is partly dissolved by powerful **stomach acids**, and churned into a kind of liquid sludge.

# Ewww. So then that sludge goes into your blood?

Good guess. The nutrients from food *do* have to end up in your bloodstream eventually. But the stomach doesn't really absorb nutrients. It's just a bag, where food and water is held and mixed – a bit like a blender.

The sludge that emerges from the stomach (called **chyme**) moves from the stomach to your **intestines**. On the way there, it oozes past the **liver** and **gallbladder**, which squirt **bile** into it via the **bile duct**. **Bile** contains more powerful enzymes, which break down the **fats** and **proteins** in food, so they can be more easily absorbed in the body.

The actual **absorption** happens in your guts – in the **small intestine** and **large intestine**. The long, thin **small intestine** gets most of the **nutrients** out, while the shorter, wider **large intestine** gets most of the **water** out. Both nutrients and water are **sucked out** (or more accurately, **pumped and filtered out**) of the gut by millions of tiny proteins in the furry, knobbly walls of the intestines. From there, they move into the bloodstream, via thousands of tiny blood vessels which wrap around the intestines.

# The Digestive System

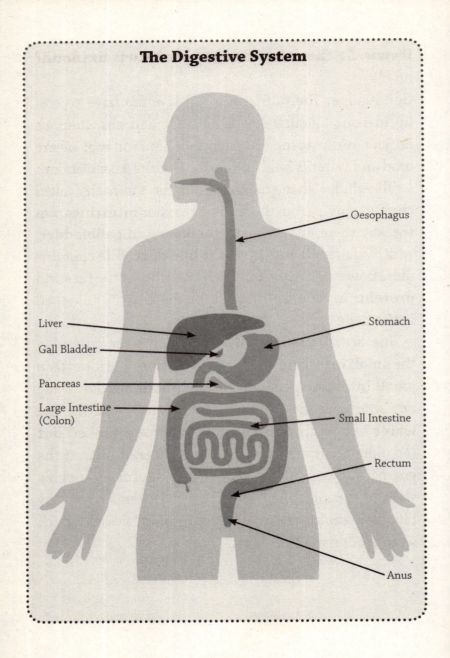

Oesophagus

Liver

Gall Bladder

Pancreas

Large Intestine
(Colon)

Stomach

Small Intestine

Rectum

Anus

## Hmmm. What happens if it *can't* suck the water out?

Good question. This does happen sometimes when we eat bad or rotten food. Or when we eat food that we are **allergic** to. In both cases, the walls of the intestines can **swell up** and **stop pumping**, leaving too much water in your gut. The result? Soggy gut-sludge that squirts and sprays uncontrollably from your bottom. Variously known as **the runs**, **the plops**, or more properly – **diarrhoea**.

## Hahahaha! Yuck!

Yuck, indeed. Thankfully, that only usually happens when we are **sick** – or when we are **made sick** by eating dodgy food or water. If you are otherwise healthy, and all goes well, then the water and nutrients are sucked out of the intestines, and the sludge that remains gets dried out into solid, chunky **faeces** (i.e. poo). These then make their way to the **rectum**, where they can be pushed out of your body in a more orderly, civilized fashion.

**So where does the water go after that, once it leaves the intestine? Straight to your wee-hole?**

Not quite. If it went *straight* to the exit at this point, you would be **weeing all day, every day**. Also, you need to filter out any dangerous **bacteria** that might have been hiding out in your food. And you need to extract all the nutrients and water you need before squirting the excess back out of your body.

From your intestines, water and nutrients move to the **liver**, **spleen**, and **pancreas** – which work together to **filter** the water and nutrients before passing them into the **bloodstream**.

From there, the **bloodstream** channels the water and nutrients around the body, nourishing and powering your **brain**, **heart**, and **lungs**, powering your muscles, and providing the building blocks needed to grow new **tissues**, like **bones**, **skin** – even **hair**.

**Okay – so *then* the water goes to your wee-hole?**

After one or two more stops, yes. As the water and nutrients and energy are used up, waste products are passed into the blood, and nutrients, water, and harmful waste materials are all sloshing through the bloodstream at once. So in one final digestive act, blood is passed through the **kidneys**, which **filter** the blood once again – capturing **nutrients**, reclaiming some **water**, and passing **waste materials**, **toxins**, and **excess water** to the **bladder** for temporary storage.

When the bladder becomes **full**, you feel an urge to wee. The wastewater moves from your bladder, through a tube called the **urethra**, at the end of which . . .

## . . . is your wee-hole?

. . . is your wee-hole, yes. With this, food and water have made their way through your entire digestive system, and you live to work, play, and poo another day.

## Woo-hoo!

That's why we seem to eat and drink so much, only to poo (and wee) those things out again. The things we pass out are not the same things that went in, and your digestive system is responsible for making sure you keep everything your body needs to stay healthy.

Of course, a healthy body also depends on the **type** and **quality of food** you eat, the **amount of food** you eat, and **how you treat your body** on a daily basis. Your body is an amazing moving, thinking, digesting machine. But how well you **maintain** it is up to you . . .

## QUICK ONES –
# DIET, LIFESTYLE, AND DISEASE

**Why can't we just live on pizza and sweets?**

Because human bodies need a wide range of nutrients to stay healthy, and you can't get them all from pizza and sweets alone. A healthy diet has a good mixture of **macronutrients**, and a full range of **micronutrients**. **Macronutrients** include **carbohydrates** (sugary and starchy foods, including bread, rice, and pasta), **fats** (animal fats, plant oils, fatty nuts), and **proteins** (from meat, eggs, fish, or plant sources). **Micronutrients** include **vitamins** (e.g vitamins A, C, D, $B_6$, $B_{12}$) and **minerals** (potassium, selenium, magnesium).

Most **sweets** are pure sugar and fat, with very little protein and no vitamins or minerals to speak of. **Pizza** features a bready (carbohydrate) base, topped with sugary tomato sauce and fatty cheese. Depending on what you top it with, there may be varying amounts of protein on top. But generally speaking, the stuff we love to lob on a pizza – ham, pepperoni, extra cheese – just adds more fat, and lacks a full range of *healthy* fats, proteins, vitamins and minerals.

If you absolutely *had to* – say, you crashed on a desert island in an aeroplane loaded with junk food – you could probably survive on pizza and sweets for a year or so. But after a while, the lack of proteins and vitamins would leave you weak, pale, and sickly. Eventually, you would likely suffer problems like **rickets** (bendy bones) and **anaemia** (a decrease in working red blood cells, which leaves you tired, lightheaded, and breathless). Not fun.

So to stay healthy, you should eat a **balanced diet** that includes plenty of **whole foods** (from plants, fish, or animals), a good range of **vitamins** (fruits and veggies generally take care of those), and a good balance of healthy **sugars**, **starches**, **oils**, and **proteins**.

Pizza and sweets once in a while are fine. But too much of *anything* will be bad for you.

## Why do all the 'bad for you' foods taste so good?

Many so-called 'junk' foods – like fizzy drinks, hot dogs, and chocolate bars are not really foods at all. They are super-processed 'food products' loaded with huge amounts of **sugar**, **salt**, and **saturated fat**. Eating too much sugar can **rot teeth** and cause **unhealthy weight gain** and **kidney disease**. Eating too much salt and fat can leave you with **high blood pressure**, **clogged arteries**, and a high chance of having a **stroke** or **heart attack**.

The problem is, high-fat, high-salt, and high-sugar junk foods often taste *great*. This is because our bodies need *some* sugar, salt, and fat to keep running, and our taste buds and appetites evolved to reward us when we found sugary, salty, fatty foods.

But there is a *big* difference between eating a sweet pineapple and eating a super-sweet chocolate bar. Pineapples contain **natural fruit sugars** and **plant fibres**, **vitamins (A and C)**, and a good amount of the healthy minerals **calcium** and **iron**. Chocolate bars contain **artificial flavourings**, and **chemically altered plant oils**. One **nourishes** your body, while the other is a fake bag of foodie tricks, which cons your brain and taste-buds into thinking it is a super-nutritious food. The same goes for naturally salty **pistachio nuts**, versus super-salty **french fries**. Or savoury hot dogs.

**Why do we have to exercise?**

Regular exercise is very important for your body, as without it, you become weak, feeble, and easily injured.

Muscles and bones grow constantly from birth, and how big and strong they get depends partly on how you *use* them.

The body is very clever, and is constantly trying to figure out what you need from it, and where it should spend the nutrients and energy you get from food. When you avoid exercise for days on end – say, skipping walks, bike rides, and physical sports in favour of playing video games – you are actually sending a signal to your brain that says, 'I don't need strong bones or muscles'. Hearing this, the brain says 'right-o', and stores the energy as **fat**, and allows your bones to become **brittle**, and your muscles to **waste away** (or **atrophy**) into wimpy sinews.

Worse yet, your **heart** and **lungs** start to atrophy without exercise, too. Which means you get tired more easily, find it harder to breathe, and feel like you never have any energy. Finally – and not many people realize this – **exercise also helps to build your brain**. Exercise builds a better supply of blood and oxygen to the brain, and forms richer, more complex networks of branching brain cells, making you better at learning and remembering new things, and better at creative thinking. So whether you want to be an athlete, an astronaut, an architect, or an accountant – exercise makes you better at *everything*.

## Why are drugs bad?

This can be a confusing question, as 'drug' can mean any substance you put into your body which creates a change (or effect) in your body or brain. By that definition, all **foods** and **medicines** are drugs, as are deadly **poisons** and **toxins**. So drugs can be helpful, harmful, or anywhere in between.

That said, when you hear about 'drugs being bad for you', this usually refers to the type of drug that is **a substance your body doesn't need**, **taken just for fun**, rather than for medical reasons. Things like **alcohol**, **tobacco**, or **medicines meant for someone else**.

All of these cause some kind of harm to the body. Alcohol, for example, **kills brain cells**, and **tobacco** causes **lung cancer**. When taken **too often** (or taken **too much at once** – something called an **overdose**), drugs can make you very sick, even kill you.

In general, it is best to avoid swallowing, smoking, or injecting *anything* into your body that isn't food or medicine – especially when you don't know what it could do to you. And never let *anyone* convince you to take a drug, just because they did. It's just not worth the risk.

**Do video games make you smart or stupid?**

Probably **neither**. Maybe a little of **both**. It likely depends on what kind of games you play, and how much time you spend playing them.

Video games definitely change your brain and body. On the one hand, some types of video game – especially **strategy games** and **complex**, **multiplayer games** – seem to increase **spatial skills** and your ability to **focus** for long periods of time. On the other hand, some video games can become **addictive** – making you irritable or anxious when you don't get to play, and making everything else seem less interesting and fun. Finally, skipping physical **exercise** and **group play** in favour of **playing video games alone** seems to be making some kids **less fit and healthy** and **lonelier**, compared to kids who play outside and together.

So the answer seems to be this: video games are probably fine, provided that you a) don't play **too often**, b) don't play for **too long** in a single session, c) play them **mostly with others**, rather than alone, and d) make time every day for **real-life**, **physical play** with friends as well. That way, you get all the fun and most of the benefits, but without the harmful effects. Game on!

# TRY IT YOURSELF:
# MAP YOUR OWN DIGESTIVE SYSTEM

Think about what you have learned about the digestive system from this chapter, then take a piece of paper, trace the image opposite and label each part of your digestive system.

Include everything from your teeth to your bum and all the in-between parts too!

To illustrate food moving through the digestive system, glue some dried pasta or cereal on various parts of your drawing – moving down the oesophagus, liquifying in the stomach, or becoming solidified in the intestines.

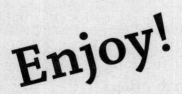

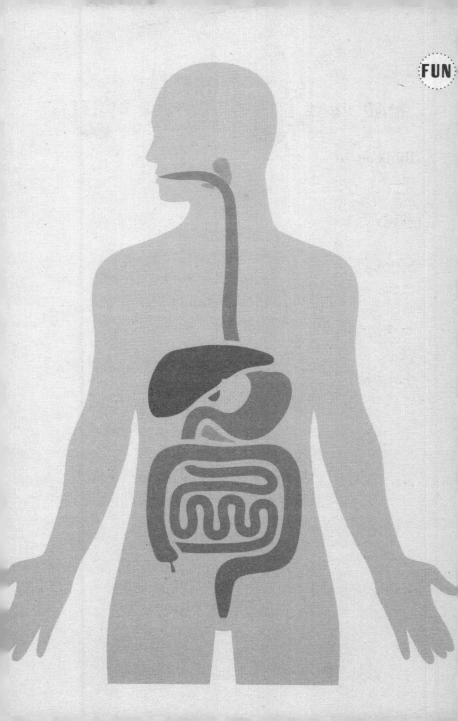

**Glenn Murphy** wrote his first book, *Why is Snot Green?*, while working at the Science Museum, London. Since then he has written around twenty popular-science titles aimed at kids and teens, including the bestselling *How Loud Can You Burp?* and *Space: The Whole Whizz-Bang Story*.

His books are read by brainy children, parents and teachers worldwide, and have been translated into Dutch, German, Spanish, Turkish, Finnish, Chinese, Japanese, Korean and Indonesian, which is kind of awesome. In 2007 he moved to the United States and began writing full-time, which explains why he now says things like 'kind of awesome'.

These days he lives in sunny, leafy North Carolina with his wife Heather, and his son Sean, who asks many marvellous questions.

**Al Murphy** has drawn pictures for lots of people, including the *Guardian*, the *New York* magazine and the *BBC*, but his favourite thing to do is draw for fun while listening to music and eating chocolate. He likes tomato soup with melted cheese and takes his tea with milk and one sugar.

**FOR CURIOUS KIDS**

SPECTACULAR SCIENCE FOR 8 YEAR OLDS

ILLUSTRATED BY AL MURPHY

**GLENN MURPHY**

BY THE AUTHOR OF *WHY IS SNOT GREEN?*

# Could we ever bring dinosaurs back to life?

# What are atoms made of?

# How do plants know where to grow?

# Why are brains all wrinkly?

**Glenn Murphy**, author of
*Why Is Snot Green?* and *How Loud Can You Burp?*,
is back to answer these and a lot of other brilliant
questions in this wonderfully funny and fascinating book –
packed with all of the science, medicine and engineering
an 8 year old needs to know.